"Don't Get So Upset!"

"Don't Get So UpSeT!"

Help Young Children Manage Their
Feelings by Understanding Your Own

Tamar Jacobson, PhD

Redleaf Press®
www.redleafpress.org
800-423-8309

Published by Redleaf Press
10 Yorkton Court
St. Paul, MN 55117
www.redleafpress.org

First edition 2008
Cover design by Lightbourne
Cover photographs by Steve Wewerka
Interior typeset in Sabon and designed by Mayfly Design
Interior photo courtesy of the author
Printed in the United States of America

The excerpts on pages 21, 23, 24, and 25 are from *Unsmiling Faces: How Preschools Can Heal,*
2nd ed. Edited by Lesley Koplow. Copyright © 2007 by Teachers College, Columbia University.
Reprinted with permission from Teachers College Press.

The poem on page 73 is from *Guide My Feet: Prayers and Meditations on Loving and Working
for Children* by Marian Wright Edelman. Copyright © 1995 by Marian Wright Edelman.
Reprinted with permission from Beacon Press, Boston.

The excerpts on pages 91–92, 93–94, and 100–101 are from *The Truth Will Set You Free: Overcoming Emotional Blindness and Finding Your True Adult Self* by Alice Miller. Copyright ©
2001 by Alice Miller. Reprinted with permission from the Perseus Book Group.

The poem excerpt on page 105 is from "Little Gidding" in *Four Quartets.* Copyright © 1942 by
T. S. Eliot and renewed 1970 by Esmé Valerie Eliot. Reprinted with permission from Houghton
Mifflin Harcourt Publishing Company.

The poem on page 158 is from *There's a Hole in My Sidewalk: The Romance of Self-Discovery*
by Portia Nelson. Copyright © 1993 by Portia Nelson. Reprinted with permission from Beyond
Words Publishing, Inc., Hillsboro, Oreg.

Library of Congress Cataloging-in-Publication Data

Jacobson, Tamar.
    "Don't get so upset!" : help young children manage their feelings by understanding your own /
Tamar Jacobson. — 1st ed.
      p. cm.
    ISBN 978-1-933653-53-2
    1. Emotions. 2. Emotions in children. 3. Child rearing. 4. Parent and child.
  I. Title.
  BF531.J32 2008
  152.4—dc22
                                    2008015690

Printed on acid-free paper

I dedicate this book to Rami Bar Giora, my psychology professor in Jerusalem, who introduced me to Haim Ginott when I was twenty-two years old,

 AND

To my mother, Beryl Kate Salis Liberman, who wrote to me a few years ago:

I always knew you would be right there,
From your mother who always loved you.

"Don't Get So Upset!"

PREFACE

I look across the sea of faces in the classroom. The students look weary from coursework responsibilities that have piled up at the end of the semester. Many of these young women hold a job while they attend school full time. They plan on becoming teachers of young children. I feel no energy from them today. Everyone looks droopy, speechless, bored, tired—as if they would rather be somewhere else, anywhere but here. My course is about families and early childhood education. Today my topic is "Becoming a Parent." I ask: "If you get to choose to become a parent—that is, if it doesn't suddenly happen to you or take you by surprise—what might be the first choice or decision you make?" One young woman with sleek brown hair and clear, bright eyes raises her hand and says, "Who will be my partner?"

People start to sit up in their seats. I go on: "What characteristics would you look for in someone you choose to be a partner in parenting?" Hands shoot up. The young women are alert now. Some even seem to bounce up and down, a little impatient to share:

" Good-looking. Money. Compassionate. Generous. Will work with me as a team. Intelligent. Sense of humor. Responsible. Reliable. Similar morals, ideas, beliefs. Loves children—all children. Spontaneous. Romantic. "

So much to discuss. For example, what does each person mean by *good-looking*? A conversation ensues, and everyone agrees: tall, dark, and handsome. I recommend that they see the movie *Pride and Prejudice* if they are looking for tall, dark, and handsome, and then I become excited as I remember Keira Knightley. "The two actors are so gorgeous, I would not know who to choose!" I muse. Laughter and excitement follow. I wonder out loud, "What does 'good-looking' have to do with parenting?" Time is up. We will continue the subject next week. I still want to discuss the expectations, hopes, and dreams of becoming a parent, as well as the challenges. Cultural forces, religious beliefs, influences on our gender identity, support systems, prenatal care, giving birth, post birth adjustment—and all the complexity of becoming a parent—including the guilt that so many people feel as they become parents. Will there be time for it all? Where has the semester gone? The room feels warm with energy as I pack computer and books into my bag. Students are drifting out of the classroom, loudly chatting and laughing. "See you next week!" they call out to me as they leave.

As I walk out to my car, an autumn chill brushes my face gently. The air is clear. I remember sitting in a class thirty-five years ago at the David Yellin College of Education in Jerusalem. Back then we knew it as Seminar Bet Hakerem, one of Israel's oldest teacher education colleges. Pnina Ezra was my early childhood instructor. She seemed quite old to me at the time. I was twenty-two. I suppose she might have been the age I am now. I smile to myself at that realization. Pnina taught me to wear a big comfortable smock with large pockets to hold tissues and other necessary early childhood "stuff." She explained that when children came to hug me I would not need to pull away from their little muddied or painted hands. My clothes would be safely protected by the apron, and that way I could always be available to enfold children in my arms, close to my heart. Pnina had compassion for children. Her subject was pedagogy, the pedagogy of love and acceptance. Sitting in her class at age twenty-two, I heard her tell us that the most important step to becoming a parent is in the choosing of our partner. At the time, I was amazed by what she said—my mind was blown. In those days I bumbled and fumbled my way through life, falling in and out of love with all sorts of people. I had never imagined or considered that one of them might be the father of my child. Indeed, Pnina's words made me think differently, more carefully about who might be a suitable father of my future children.

My attention returns to the current time. I climb into my car and sit silently for a while. I wonder, "Will my students, like me, remember what we talked about today in thirty-five years' time?" I smile to myself as I start up the car. It feels good to be a professor. I look forward to seeing everyone next week.

Swami Ji Sivalingam was my yoga teacher many years ago. While we were in the middle of practicing our yoga *asanas* (postures), he would say, "So happy, so joy. This is yoga." Then, just as he had managed to convince us to maintain a difficult posture, he would call out sharply, "Keep a smiling face!" Oh, how that would make me laugh inside, and I would *feel* the joy all over my contorted body.

He once told me that each time before he started to instruct a yoga class, he would thank his past mentors and teachers. From time to time I think back to all the people I have considered teachers and mentors, and I silently thank them for their influence. After all, we are touched and affected by all those who wander onto our path, whether they come on purpose or by chance. I especially remember those who were kind and supportive to me, encouraged me in my education and those who inspired me with their work on relationships and young children.

Although my memories of elementary and high school teachers are few, Mr. Tregidgo, my high school English teacher, stands out for me. I do not remember much about the lessons he taught except for learning never to start a sentence with "I." What I do remember about him, though, was his greeting: whenever he would meet me in the hallway of that old British colonial school of Rhodesia (now Zimbabwe), he would wave and smile, and say, "Shalom!" Mr. Tregidgo was not Jewish, but I was. In fact, I was the only Jewish girl in the class. Each time he greeted me in that manner I felt included, important, and worthwhile. His greeting was something personal, just for me. Here it is, more than forty years later, and I still remember him for that.

I first heard Bruce Perry speak at a national conference about five years ago. It was a life-altering experience. Every piece of his talk resonated with my life's work as an early childhood teacher. The discussion about brain development was extremely exciting, for Perry talked about emotional memory templates and the importance of relationships. Each moment during his presentation became an "Aha!" experience for me, reinforcing and reconfirming everything I have been thinking, feeling, and experiencing about working with young children, their families, and their teachers. And it also helped to explain what I had been uncovering about myself in therapy over the years. I have since heard Bruce Perry speak four or five times, and each time I have the same experience.

He inspires me to continue the work I do and expands my understanding of my own emotional development. It is definitely people like him who remind me how important my work is. Bruce Perry says it is all about relationships.

I must admit that I most likely am not only a teacher but also a mentor for others. The wheel of life spins on, and my awareness of that leads me to think about what sorts of pieces of myself or my life experiences might have served as examples for others searching for their way. We can never really know which action or word spoken to others affects them. Every person's needs are related to where he or she is, at different places in time and experience. But, at the very least, we can offer ourselves generously and openly to others, sharing our most vulnerable selves, and being as authentic and honest as we are able.

Thank you to my son, Gilad Barkan, for having the courage to tell me how he feels, and to my husband, Tom Jacobson, for having the courage to hear how I feel. I am truly blessed to have these two wonderful men in my life. Thank you to Redleaf Press, namely Linda Hein and David Heath, for supporting this book. It is a dream come true, for I have been thinking about emotional development for more than thirty years and wanting to write a book like this for a decade. A special thanks to Deanne Kells, my editor. You understood exactly what I was trying to say and guided me to (in your words) "make the book shine forth in all its glory and give the reader a sense of real actions that might help us all 'follow in Tamar's footsteps,' albeit on our own paths."

INTRODUCTION

This is one aspect of teaching that I hadn't thought of until now—the emotional power teachers have over children.

—Colleen, undergraduate student

Too often, caregivers are given the message that there are "correct" emotions to feel; emotions must be controlled or regulated. Language such as "over-attached," "cares too much," "don't get too involved" all suggest that there is a correct amount of emotion. Once we care for someone and care about them, our heart is involved. We cannot measure the caring and concern.

—Enid Elliott

Early Emotional Memories Last Forever

Very early one morning, at the conclusion of a national conference, I shared a taxi to the airport with a colleague, another early childhood teacher educator. We discussed what I would be writing about in my next book. I shared that my topic was how teachers' emotions affect their interactions with children, especially in response to what they consider challenging behaviors. She was silent for a moment and then said reflectively, "I often think that people who work with young children have been emotionally wounded when they were children themselves. It's almost as if they have chosen the profession of early care and education because of that." I thought about what she said and recognized that through the years as a teacher and professor I certainly have learned and come to understand much about my own childhood experiences and inner self through observing and interacting with children and their families.

As part of the ongoing process of exploring my inner life, I have learned to notice patterns of thought or feelings, and when or how they occur, so that I might understand myself better. For example, I have realized that I swing between feelings of being in and out of confidence. Knowing my confidence state is a good barometer for me. It helps me to know how to take on a challenge or survive a difficult day.

Understanding myself certainly enhances and enriches my life. But this is not the only reason I have undertaken this exploration. At one point in my early twenties I realized that my interactions and behaviors with young children could affect them for the rest of their lives. At the time I was reading Haim Ginott's book *Between Parent and Child: New Solutions to Old Problems* (Ginott 1969) for a child psychology course. It was while I was reading about how it is not good to tease children that I realized teasing had always felt hurtful when I was a child.

While children are playful, it does not mean they are not serious. In fact, their play is serious indeed. They are learning about life through their play, and they take seriously what the significant adults in their lives say to them. They have to—after all, children depend on adults for their survival, emotionally and physically. When we tease young children or use sarcastic humor, they most often believe our words to be true. A child's sense of humor is not yet developed and sophisticated like an adult's. It is crucial to respect children and not to trivialize them with teasing and sarcasm. It is critical to take them seriously by validating and acknowledging their feelings. Children need to know what we really think about them almost as much as they need the air they breathe. They might lead us to believe they understand our humor in order to please us. In fact, our humor is often confusing and sometimes hurtful to children.

As a child I learned to laugh along with my stepfather, mother, and brother when they made fun of me, my ideas, or even people who were important to me, including my father, who did not live with us. It seemed to be the way members of my family expressed love—through teasing and sarcasm. So I laughed along. I also learned to believe that what they were saying was reality. Deep inside, I was hurt and confused. Ginott explains this phenomenon in his book, which I read while studying to become a preschool and kindergarten teacher in Israel. I remember that as I read his words, I wept with relief. I felt validated. More than that, I learned that I was not abnormal for having been hurt and confused by the teasing, which created in me an immediate longing for sincere, authentic, serious loving. Looking back, I realized that my interactions as a child with significant adults in my life had affected me for a very long time. I was amazed. It was a revelation! It hit me hard and deep: whatever I would do and say with and to young children could have a profound effect on them. The responsibility became immediately awesome.

So, back in 1970, I began an exploration of my inner life in order to understand why I do what I do so that when I was interacting with young children I could be my most authentic self. The journey never ends. It has been excruciating at times and, at others, exhilarating and revealing. My exploration has made me feel uncomfortable and has occasionally caused members of my family and some of my friends discomfort too. But finding out how I came to be me is not some kind of self-indulgent, navel-gazing, egotistical preoccupation. It is my responsibility as a teacher.

Self-awareness helps me prevent inappropriate actions and reactions. For example, I am inclined to tease children because that is what I experienced as a child. But I am still able to stop myself, put myself in their shoes, and speak clearly and with respect. This is because I am aware that teasing was confusing and hurtful for me and made me feel helpless.

What to Do with Children's Behaviors That Challenge Us

Behavior management, including discipline, seems to be a popular topic these days. More than that, teachers and caregivers seem starved for information about it. In a recent survey of student teachers, in which my university's teacher education department asked how it might improve the student teaching experience, 100 percent of the students replied that they needed more behavior management strategies. Indeed, one of my colleagues says, "It's *all* about behavior management." During my workshops and presentations about discipline at conferences and in-service trainings, I have hardly managed to complete the introduction when teachers of young children begin to ask for solutions and answers. They ask me for strategies and prescriptions. They want me to tell them exactly what to do when a child bites, hits, refuses to clean up, answers back, throws a tantrum, or does not follow directions. Many express feeling helpless or frustrated with young children's behaviors they consider challenging.

Usually I start off a workshop or presentation by asking participants or students to describe how they were disciplined as young children. We write the list of punishments on the board or flipchart and uncover that most of the attendees experienced some kind of pain or humiliation when they were young children. Parents have scolded, slapped, pinched, yelled at, or threatened them—and those were the milder punishments! Many in the audience express resentment from these experiences.

I cannot help but wonder how those earliest memories have affected the very people who will be disciplining children in their care. At a recent in-service training of early childhood teachers, we talked deeply and sincerely about the way we were disciplined and how it affects our behaviors in the classroom. I watched teachers and caregivers as they bared their deepest fears and anxieties, some weeping as they realized how many of these feelings were affecting their classroom management strategies and, more importantly, their sometimes misguided perceptions about children. It was powerful, and I was inspired by their courage. Like many teachers, I want to give children what I never had. For others, their early childhood memories about discipline are satisfactory enough that they want to repeat what they experienced. Clearly, our own emotional development in childhood, or ways we were guided or punished, affects how we feel about what to do with children whose behaviors challenge us.

In *The Emotional Development of Young Children: Building an Emotion-Centered Curriculum*, Marilou Hyson describes the dangers of neglecting emotions. After reviewing the research about young children's emotions, she summarizes several points, including that emotions guide and motivate behavior "from infancy throughout life," and that all emotions, whether negative or positive, are important for development. Hyson goes on to say:

> " An underlying message of all this research is that emotional development is too important to be left to chance. *Adults, including early childhood professionals, can make the difference, supporting positive development, being alert to possible problems, and intervening early and effectively.* "
> (italics mine; Hyson 2004, 9–10)

Ever since beginning my career as a preschool and kindergarten teacher, I have considered the importance of my role in supporting positive emotional development for young children. I wonder how teachers can be effective if they are not in touch with their own emotional development, for our interventions in emotional situations are crucial in supporting children toward acquiring a positive self-identity. Recently, one of my undergraduate students wrote about how she is drawn to children with levels of self-confidence similar to hers as a child:

> " When I was in elementary school . . . I always felt that I was not good enough and did not have the slightest bit of self-confidence. Having grown up feeling that way, I vowed

to make sure I would find the ones who have low self-esteem like I did and take them under my wings to show them that there is nothing to fear and that they are capable of many things. Because I still have many doubts and reservations about my abilities, I can detect others who share similar feelings. "

If we are not aware of what frightens or concerns us or causes us anxiety, if we do not know our emotional limitations, we might not be as supportive as we would like to be. We might, in fact, unintentionally shame a child the way we were shamed as children. Therefore I want to emphasize an extra dimension to the concept of behavior management. It is an aspect we need to support our important work of appropriate interventions in emotional situations: self-reflection about what makes us *adults* tick emotionally.

Reflective Practice

The National Association for the Education of Young Children (NAEYC) expects professionals to engage in reflective practice (NAEYC 1993). Teachers are encouraged to cultivate certain specific attitudes toward reflective thinking, such as open-mindedness, wholeheartedness, and responsibility for facing the consequences. There is evidence that reflective practice enhances change in classroom practice. Much of the research about reflective practice looks at teachers' ability to assess a situation and make sense out of the experience. Teachers who reflect on how they feel and why they feel the way they do are in a better position to understand their interactions with others. The idea of self-awareness is discussed as assisting teachers in their classroom practices and personal lives. Teachers have control over the decisions they make, yet without their active involvement, autonomy, and reflection, it is difficult to make changes in classroom practice (Jacobson 2003).

Research about the importance of healthy emotional development has confirmed what I have been uncovering about *my own* emotional development and how *I* feel. It has helped me understand how and why I might have struggled with my relationships, professional or personal, these past fifty-eight years or so. Research has especially helped me to understand and improve my relationships with young children, families, and teachers. Throughout this book I share some of these self-uncoverings, in the hope that they will encourage you to embark on your own self-exploration.
As we learn more about ourselves, we are able to understand more clearly why we do what we do, especially when faced with children's challenging behaviors. This book will not give you my prescriptions for the best ways to manage children's behaviors. I do discuss interventions *that worked for me* and that might be appropriate for you to use as well. But mostly I recommend that you find your own strategies that fit your comfort level. This will depend on how you were disciplined as a child, what your beliefs are, or what kinds of behaviors cause you discomfort and why. What has worked for me may not necessarily work for you. Our life experiences, earliest childhood memories, ways in which significant adults in our life interacted with us, and problem-solving techniques are likely to be quite different.

Overview of the Book

I begin by discussing some of the research on children's emotional development (chapter 1). Brain researchers explain that emotional memory stored in the brain during the first four or five years of life is un-erasable. The ways in which we interact with young children affect their future emotional development and how they acquire a self-identity. The literature tells us that meaningful, loving relationships are crucial in young children's emotional development.

Understanding how we feel and why—by taking a look at ourselves—is the theme of the second chapter, where I discuss different kinds of feelings that affect our interactions in emotional situations with children. In chapter 3, I explore feelings related to anger more specifically, because anger causes many people some form of discomfort. In a survey about anger that I conducted in the spring of 2006, teachers in campus children's centers reported feelings of confusion or expressed a fear of being out of control as part of their own anger experiences. In a study about scolding in child care across the United States, Denmark, China, and Japan, Erik Sigsgaard writes about why adults scold children. One of the reasons is simply because the adults themselves were spanked or scolded as children (Sigsgaard 2005). Pre-service teachers and teachers at in-service trainings tell me, time and again, how resentful or angry they still feel, years later, when they recall feeling humiliated while being scolded as young children.

In addition to being affected by intense emotions like anger, our interactions are influenced when we feel empowered. Therefore, in chapter 4, "We Face Our Feelings of Powerlessness," I continue the discussion from "In and Out of Confidence," chapter 4 in my first book, *Confronting Our Discomfort: Clearing the Way for Anti-Bias in Early Childhood* (Jacobson 2003). Classroom management, discipline, and the way we see ourselves controlling our domain are also connected to different power issues. For example, in what ways does the power structure of our profession influence our self-identity? How did we come to choose the profession of early care and education? Put even more simply, how do we empower children when we do not feel powerful or confident ourselves? For example, allowing children to speak out or make a stand for themselves can feel inappropriate, even intimidating, when we have difficulties being assertive ourselves.

Having confronted some uncomfortable emotions and discussed some of our inappropriate interventions, I turn in chapter 5 to the question of why we do what we do, as we claim our childhood traumas large and small. This chapter leads us into self-reflection. By creating a type of internal ethnography, or qualitative study of ourselves, which I call "researching the self," we begin by taking a look at our own emotional history. In doing so, we become aware of what makes us uncomfortable in children's emotional situations, and we understand how the discipline we received as young children affects our interventions and interactions with behaviors we consider challenging.

As we are repeatedly tested with our responses in emotional situations, we also come to know ourselves more deeply. Once we create a foundation of self, where we are on the road to confronting, understanding, and accepting our own emotions, we are in a better position to think about practical applications of discipline strategies in the classroom. In the sixth chapter, I discuss setting limits, what to do about tantrums, and how to meet our expectations to create safe emotional environments for ourselves as well as the children. I also take a look at the difference between discipline and punishment. By applying strategies that do not humiliate, punish, or scold, we learn, as children and adults, to accept the negative as well as the positive aspects of all our emotions.

In the final chapter, "We Can Change Our Emotional Scripts," I talk about telling the story of our emotional history. Hyson tells us that children's emotional development is too important to be left to chance (Hyson 2004). But what about the teachers who are expected to guide and support children as they develop a positive emotional identity and become socially competent citizens of the world? Bruce Perry emphasizes that we have the choice to develop humane children, starting from their earliest years, by giving them strong, repetitive, positive emotional memories (Perry 2007). How do we do that if we never experienced humane treatment while growing up? The emotional development of *teachers*, therefore, is too important to be left to chance. Indeed, in the late 1950s and the 1960s, teacher educators suggested that:

- teacher preparation should involve a development of awareness about their emotional life;
- human emotional qualities are at the core of teaching;
- and the very behavior of teachers is a product of their emotional self-identity. (Jacobson 2003)

It takes courage to confront our emotions and realize that some of the ways we were treated as children affect how we perceive those behaviors we consider challenging in young children. In many cases it is not so much that a particular child has behavior problems. In fact, often it has to do with how we *perceive* those behaviors in connection with how we remember being treated as young children, or how we observed our peers being managed with similar problems. Indeed, it is all about our relationships with one another.

This book is for you, about you and me—the adults who care for and educate young children. Whether you are a student preparing to become an early childhood teacher, a beginning or veteran teacher of young children, or a teacher educator, this book is intended to help you uncover your own feelings as you try to manage children's behaviors and think about strategies that might work for you. It is meant to serve as a guide for your own self-reflection, rather than yet another set of instructions about *the right way to do it*—external strategies or techniques designed to fix children's behavior problems.

Many years ago a friend gave me a poster featuring words written by Haim Ginott, the child psychologist I wrote about earlier, who had influenced me in the early 1970s. I still have these words hanging up in my office. They accompany me as I work with families, children, and their teachers. I give them out to everyone I know, and I share them with you now.

> " I've come to a frightening conclusion. I am the decisive
> element in the classroom. It is my personal approach that
> creates the climate. It is my daily mood that makes the
> weather. As a teacher I possess tremendous power to make
> a child's life miserable or joyous. I can be a tool of torture
> or an instrument of inspiration. I can humiliate or humor,
> hurt or heal. In all situations it is my response that decides
> whether a crisis will be escalated or deescalated and a child
> humanized or dehumanized. "   (Ginott 1972)

Being a teacher of young children is the most powerful profession I know. It comes with an awesome responsibility: it is up to us to offer children different options, new ways to solve problems, models of kindness and compassion, and relationships that will reinforce and develop a strong, positive emotional self-identity. So many times I have looked into the eyes of a child who is angry, bewildered, or frustrated, or who has given up the fight altogether, and I see myself, recognize those feelings, or remember the anxiety from somewhere deep in my own childhood psyche. Have we forgotten so soon that once we were children too?

References

Elliot, E. 2007. *We're not robots: The voices of day care providers.* New York: State University of New York Press.

Ginott, H. G. 1969. *Between parent and child: New solutions to old problems.* New York: Macmillan.

Ginott, H. G. 1972. *Teacher & child: A book for parents and teachers.* New York: Macmillan.

Hyson, M. 2004. *The emotional development of young children: Building an emotion-centered curriculum.* 2nd ed. New York: Teachers College Press.

Jacobson, T. 2003. *Confronting our discomfort: Clearing the way for anti-bias in early childhood.* Portsmouth, N.H.: Heinemann.

National Association for the Education of Young Children (NAEYC). 1993. A conceptual framework for early childhood professional development: A position statement of the National Association for the Education of Young Children. *Young Children* 49 (3): 68–77.

Perry, B. D. 2007. *Early childhood and brain development: How experience shapes child, community and culture.* DVD. ChildTrauma Academy.

Sigsgaard, E. 2005. *Scolding: Why it hurts more than it helps.* Trans. D. H. Silver. New York: Teachers College Press.

CHAPTER ONE

WE CREATE POSITIVE EMOTIONAL ENVIRONMENTS FOR CHILDREN

Our brains are starving for relationships. Our children are starved for relationships. The whole culture is touch deprived—relational deprived.

—BRUCE PERRY

About a year ago, I received an e-mail from a reader of my blog, which I have been writing for the past three years:

> I'm a parent of a 2-year-old boy and would love to read any books you may have written, essays, articles, speeches—EVERYTHING you have ever said on the topic of early childhood. . . . There are so few approaches to early childhood that [have] basic kindness as a point of departure. I call it, 'I'm-on-your-side-ness' and sometimes that

translates into 'even-if-I-don't-understand-you-now-I'll-
never-ever-stop-trying-to.' "

Driving back and forth to work, I thought about this e-mail.
It occurred to me that the parenting styles that swaddled me as a
child were far from kind. Indeed, I do not recall feeling the "I'm-
on-your-side-ness" that the writer described, except, perhaps, from
my father. He did not live with me, but I visited him every two
weeks. He was in his sixties by the time I was five years old, more
like a grandfather than a father figure. A gentle, soft-spoken man
who expressed delight at my achievements, my father related to my
intellectual ability. For example, when I entered high school, he sent
me a *Cassell's Compact French-English English-French Dictionary*,
which I have kept to this day. My older siblings were not around
me much. My oldest sister left home by the time I was six or seven,
and the second-oldest sister was mostly at boarding school and
then went away to Europe as soon as she was able. When I was
twelve, my brother left Rhodesia for college in England, and my
mother gave me a framed photograph of him as a special gift when
we returned from the airport. In order to gain acknowledgment and
respect from my mother, I learned that my brother was a very important person—someone to be noticed and listened to.

I would have to say that I experienced significant parenting
models from a number of people in my family—namely, my mother,
stepfather, and older brother. Their styles were similar. They used
criticism, sarcasm, teasing, name calling, threatening, ostracizing,
and labeling. Their methods included anything from laughing at
my developing beliefs, ideas, and emotions to sneering at what I
was doing and how I looked. Ironically, both the significant men in
my life as I grew up (stepfather and brother) were also those from

whom I longed for acknowledgment the most. Yet, instead, they were both sarcastic and teased me.

As I considered the e-mail from the blog reader, I thought, "How on earth did I learn that basic kindness and I'm-on-your-side-ness are a point of departure for interacting with young children?" I certainly do not practice it on myself. Instead, right up to today, I struggle with reproaching myself scathingly for everything I do, feel, or accomplish—and certainly for how I look. As I look back, I shudder at the thought that I might have treated others, including my own son, like that. And yet, somewhere deep inside me, I know that basic kindness is, most certainly, a point of departure for the way we treat young children. Where, oh where, did it come from? I had to assume that I intuitively learned from the kindness of strangers over and over again. Strangers were always being kind to me: mothers of playmates; school or college teachers over the years; the nuns at the Mater Dei Hospital back in Bulawayo, Rhodesia, where I was born; youth leaders; therapists; friends. The list is endless, yet the people's qualities are always the same: listening, accepting, validating my emotional experience, giving me their time, telling or showing me love in concrete ways, believing me, giving me permission to express sorrow and anger, allowing and delighting in me just being me.

Many people choose to replicate parenting models even when they are abusive, and some decide not to. I chose to use the hopeful, kind interactions of strangers and mentors as my guide, an antidote to what I was learning about myself at home. I do not know why or how I did that. Was it a type of resilience I developed or perhaps inherited genetically? As I answered that e-mail in my mind, I said, "Yes, I'm-on-your-side-ness is crucial for helping young children develop those kinds of emotional memories that will create kind and humane adults, as well as strengthen their self-confidence. I know it from deep inside my soul. What if all those strangers and mentors had not reached out their hands, souls, smiles, lives to me? I would have felt so alone, lost, and abandoned. Who knows where I might have ended up?"

Once again, I sensed the kindness of strangers from a woman's e-mail sharing her support for my work. It gave me much to think about, organize, and focus on as I wrote this book, especially as I wrote about adults' emotional reactions to children's expressions of feelings—reminding me about the work I do with teachers of young children as I try to convince them about basic kindness and I'm-on-your-side-ness as playing significant roles in young children's emotional development.

HEALTHY EMOTIONAL DEVELOPMENT IN CHILDREN IS VERY IMPORTANT.

What We Know about Emotional Development

Many early childhood teachers and caregivers would probably agree with me that we have never really needed research to tell us that children's social-emotional development affects their academic success and emotional competence. Any early childhood professional knows that children who feel good about themselves are able to focus on cognitive tasks with more ease than children who are troubled, anxious, angry, tired, or sad. Children who are able to play in a cooperative, give-and-take fashion and who get along with others are just happier than those who seem alone, excluded, or unpopular. Therefore, it is reinforcing and affirming to discover from the recent brain development literature that what we felt intuitively for so many years is now backed up by scientific research. Indeed, researchers, educators, psychologists, social workers, and people from disciplines outside of early childhood education are producing evidence that can support our relationships with young children in our classrooms.

"We have in fact arrived at a moment in which different disciplines are converging to produce a new understanding of emotional life" (Gerhardt 2004, 1). In *Why Love Matters: How Affection Shapes a Baby's Brain*, Sue Gerhardt describes the importance of quality relationships between caregivers and young children. Gerhardt makes us aware that the ways in which we interact with children will shape them for the rest of their lives. According to Robin Karr-Morse and Meredith Wiley, a growing body of research shows that if children are badly treated in the first two years of life, they are more likely to become violent older children and adults. They warn us that "infancy and toddlerhood are times of enormous complexity when potentials for favorable adult outcomes can be maximized, diminished, or lost" (Karr-Morse and Wiley 1997, 15).

Marilou Hyson suggests that twenty years of research should be strong enough evidence to help us realize the importance of children's emotional development, as well as the adult's role in "supporting emotional competence." Hyson summarizes the body of research with four points:

1. Emotions are the principal guides and motivators of behavior and learning from infancy throughout life.
2. Both positive and negative emotions—joy, interest, surprise, as well as sadness, anger, and fear—play important roles in development.

3. Young children's ability to express, understand, and regulate their emotions follows typical developmental sequences or pathways.
4. Both biological and environmental factors influence that pathway—temperament, culture, relationships with adults and peers, and many other factors come into play throughout childhood and beyond (Hyson 2004, 9).

Such a strong body of research should be enough evidence for us to understand the importance of children's emotional development as well as our role in supporting their social-emotional competence. We now know that both negative and positive emotions play an important role in emotional development. We need to be intentional in how we guide and motivate children's behavior and learning from the day they are born. Emotional memory in children's developing brains will be influenced not only by biological factors like genes or temperament, but just as importantly by experiences in their environment, including culture and relationships with significant adults.

The human brain is most impressionable very early in life. In fact, 85 percent of the foundational structure of the brain's functioning is developed during those very early years (Perry 2007). It follows that this is the time when humanity, compassion, and empathy can develop. From birth, our brain awaits those initial experiences that will help it to organize and allow it to express its potential. Even as a child is capable of learning language or how to transition from rolling over to sitting and from crawling to standing, her brain is organizing as a result of experiences and relationships. We learn language, we move, and—most importantly—we interpret the entire world in the context of our relationships. According to a leading expert in brain development, positive, harmonious, responsive, care-giving experiences affect the strength and solid consistency of the part of the brain that provides the trunk for our relationships for the rest of our life (Perry 2007). Without these types of experiences we will forever have relationship difficulties. According to Perry, our brain functioning is a reflection of our human experiences. For example, racism, misogyny, and ageism are human inventions. None of them are genetically determined. These attitudes come from our experiences.

> " Not only are warm and supportive teacher-child relationships associated with higher levels of social and emotional competence, greater receptivity to the school setting, and better reasoning skills that result in higher achievement during the school years, but there are indications that these important relationships can also play a part in buffering the adverse effects of stress on the developing brain. "
> (Koplow 2007, xvi)

It is up to us to create positive emotional environments for our children. The literature about emotional development clearly states time and again that it is our roles, interactions, and relationships as parents, teachers, and other significant adults in children's lives that will guide and facilitate children's acquisition of healthy social-emotional skills. Indeed, teachers are called upon to heal, guide, facilitate, model, and teach children how to regulate their emotions. What has become clear to me from all the literature about brain and emotional development, and from what all the professionals in many different fields are saying, is that *what we do matters* (Jacobson 2006). I know this because researchers and educators tell me about the early and lasting effects of children's environments and experiences on brain development. I also know this because I understand that, even at age fifty-eight, aspects of my personal and professional life are still affected by my own early childhood experiences. Therefore, the more I come to understand my own emotions, the more effective I will be in helping children manage theirs.

How Teachers' Emotional Life Is Ignored in the Field

Coincidentally, at the same time I was preparing this chapter, *Teachers College Record* invited me to review a new book, *Unsmiling Faces: How Preschools Can Heal*, a collection of essays edited by Lesley Koplow. This is an excellent example of a strategy book that I mention in the section "Read Some of the Literature for Yourself," toward the end of this chapter. It is an important book because it not only describes child development and how children are affected by relationships in the early years, but specifically talks about preschools as environments that can heal traumatized or abused children. It discusses very important issues that teachers need to understand about young children's social-emotional development and suggests what they might do when confronted by serious emotional damage in children. It is, in fact, one of many books and articles giving teachers much-needed advice about how to manage children's feelings and challenging behaviors. It does, however, leave out an important piece: for me, the book would be much more complete were it to include a chapter dedicated to emotional support for teachers who are doing this important healing work with children with special needs.

Although the book is written with a specific focus on children who have been traumatized, it is definitely appropriate and suitable for educators who work with typical children in any preschool setting. Our early childhood classrooms should *all* be emotional safe havens for *everyone*. To that point, Vivian Gussin Paley asks in the foreword, "Is there a preschool anywhere that does not include those who at times feel sad, angry, and helpless?" (Koplow 2007, vii). Paley goes on to say:

> " The rest of us, teaching in relatively stable circumstances, tend to resist the idea that some sort of therapy may be a part of our job, even as we encourage larger numbers of families and children to meet with therapists. We tell ourselves in the face of worrisome and unpredictable behaviors, 'The ordinary classroom is not meant to be a therapeutic community.' Then we go about picking up the random pieces of confused, frustrated, and otherwise unfinished development that surround us as we try to create the facsimile of a caring family. " (Koplow 2007, vii)

The writers of *Unsmiling Faces* describe in detail ways of creating a safe emotional haven for young, traumatized children, including those who are homeless and abused, and how to work with families and staff. The book is thorough and informative about the development of a child's self-concept, and it even includes discussions about the importance of play and creating the appropriate physical therapeutic environment, as well as various techniques such as play therapy. One contributor reminds us that, "if we conceive of childhood only as a carefree, joyful time, we may be denying the experiential and emotional realities of many at-risk children who enter our classroom each morning" (Koplow 2007, 17). This statement is the introduction to a chapter with the title "If You're Sad and You Know It," an antidote to the usual children's happiness song we all know so well. The author suggests that all our "attempts to 'cheer' children may convey *our own* difficulty ac-knowledging, affirming, and tolerating a range of affects in young children, including those that communicate emotional pain and dis-tress" (italics mine; Koplow 2007, 17–18). In my opinion, this may be one of the most important statements in the entire book.

The second part of the book opens with a chapter about the teacher's role. It has critical implications for teacher education in general, not only for facilitators of special education. In this piece, Judith Ferber discusses the teacher's role in a *healing* type of pre-school classroom, including details about organizing the physical environment, the importance of schedules and routines, how to set limits, and even the appropriate type of curriculum. In other words the teacher in a preschool setting has many different roles, as instructor, caregiver, and limit setter. Ferber talks about the im-portance of the teacher-child relationship, describing it as "pivotal" and the "mediating link" (Koplow 2007, 55). She goes on to say that, "Clearly, the importance of the teacher-child relationship for a needy child [I would say, *any* child] is paramount in effecting the development of cognition as well as emotional well-being" (Kop-low 2007, 56).

These insights from "If You're Sad and You Know It" lead me to question why there is a lack of discussion about teachers' emo-tions. For example, many professional counselors seek out some type of therapeutic supervision so that their feelings, beliefs, emo-tional reactions, and subjectivity might not interfere with treatment of their clients. If we are to organize and develop preschools that heal, whether for traumatized or for typical children, what are we doing, as a profession, to help teachers self-reflect specifically about how they feel in the face of *their own* "difficulty acknowledging, affirming, and tolerating a range of affects in young children, including those that communicate emotional pain and distress"? (Koplow 2007, 17–18).

Koplow states, "Teacher-child interactions must be open-ended, spontaneous, and genuine in order to facilitate emotional growth" (Koplow 2007, 24). I could not agree more. However, in this very important book about creating emotional safe havens for young children, there is not much discussion of emotional support for the teachers who work with them. Koplow goes on to say that adults can help children emotionally by giving them "permission to feel and express sadness, fear, anger, worry, and loneliness as well as joy, delight, excitement, enthusiasm, and other positive emotions" (Koplow 2007, 25). I cannot help but wonder how the adults who are caring for and educating young children are able to understand their own such emotions. More importantly, what are we, as teacher educators, doing to help them become more aware of their feelings so that they may be open-minded, spontaneous, and genuine in their relationships with children? Indeed, I have been wondering about this aspect of self-reflection for teachers for some time now. I talk about it quite a bit with relation to our biases in my previous book, *Confronting Our Discomfort: Clearing the Way for Anti-Bias in Early Childhood*, just as I discuss why reflective practice of this nature is so important for teachers:

> 66 There is no safe place emotionally or physically in the education and development of teachers for confronting uncomfortable feelings they might have. . . . It is not possible for teachers to refer children to their colleagues [like counselors do] or seek counseling supervision in the context

of education. Teachers just have to get on with it one way or another. As a result, young children are the recipients of many of our harmful, unconscious behaviors. " (Jacobson 2003, 19)

Early childhood classrooms should most certainly be safe emotional havens. The pertinent question for me is this: How might we support teachers doing this very important work with young children?

Another book on the topic of social-emotional development even goes so far as to suggest that teachers should have "mature healthy personalities" for supporting children's emotional development (Gartrell 2004). Nancy Weber, a contributor to this book about teaching social-emotional skills, goes on to say:

" Teachers who have gone into early childhood education with their own basic needs unmet, or who feel oppressed and burdened, may inadvertently draw excessively from the children to meet their own basic needs. This preoccupation with concerns of their own precludes an understanding of children, and therefore makes acting on this understanding impossible. " (Weber, in Gartrell 2004, 4)

I would think that a statement such as this would be most off-putting for any teacher trying to acquire resources to teach children social-emotional skills. Surely a teacher would feel at a loss as to how she might factor in such deep and complex emotional insecurities. In the first place, how do we define someone as having a healthy, mature personality? How long does it take to become healthy and mature? I often question my own maturity, and I have reached the ripe old age of fifty-eight! Secondly, how does this author intend to support a teacher who feels, as she describes: "oppressed and burdened" or "with basic needs unmet"? These broad statements about apparent flaws in teachers' personalities are left hanging for an educator to pass over on her way to becoming the best teacher she strives to be. Except for leaving the profession if one has these undesirable human frailties, no other solution or assistance is offered.

ACTIONS TO TAKE

Read Some of the Literature for Yourself

For the past ten years or so, I have been collecting early childhood publications that discuss managing young children's emotions or suggest guidance strategies about their behaviors. Please refer to the suggested reading section at the end of this chapter for a list of some of these resources. Some address how to handle boys, specifically, and others are about children with special needs. Some describe the importance of quality relationships in terms of influencing earliest emotional memories in the brain as well as enhancing academic success later in life. Many describe, in detail, which exact strategies to use for this or that behavior problem or issue. There are many instructive and thorough books suggesting worthwhile, positive, and appropriate approaches for teachers of young children to use in their classrooms. As you browse through some of the references at the end of this chapter, you will surely identify strategies that fit your belief system or the way you approach discipline. As you will see in the following chapters, the strategies you choose will depend on your own early childhood experiences and your beliefs, values, and educational ideologies.

Most of the books and articles prescribe a number of steps that will help solve problems you might be having with young children. For example, Dan Gartrell uses what he calls a "five finger formula" so that one of the prescribed steps can be counted from each finger (Gartrell 2004, 82). "Cool down" is for the thumb; "identifying the problem" goes with the pointer finger; "brainstorming solutions" is connected with the middle finger, which Gartrell calls "the tall guy"; and so on. In an earlier chapter, Gartrell presents six "guidance practices," including reducing the need for mistaken behavior by "using teaching practices that are developmentally appropriate and culturally sensitive," practicing "positive teacher-child relations," holding class meetings, using "positive statements of expected behaviors," and building partnerships with parents (Gartrell 2004, 31–32).

In *Social and Emotional Development*, Dave Riley and his fellow authors offer seven practical tips for interacting with infants and toddlers, all of which connect research with practice to help teachers and parents understand social and emotional development (Riley et al. 2008). Examples include responding promptly to young children's distress signals or allowing children to have transitional objects such as a favorite stuffed animal. The authors explain clearly how to foster children's impulse control:

> Instead of saying 'Don't run,' try rephrasing your request: 'Use walking feet.' Instead of 'Don't hit,' try saying, 'Soft touches.' You can take it one step further by modeling the action while saying the words. Instead of 'Don't pull the

cat's tail,' try 'Pet the kitty like this.' . . . Monitor how often you say 'don't,' and force yourself to rephrase your directives in positive terms. " (Riley et al. 2008, 72)

One of the books I read suggests six things you can do as a teacher to change your approach with children. The authors describe ways to use your body language, like smiling, touching, or hugging; how to listen attentively and what types of questions to ask; and how to "reframe [children's] statements in a positive light" (Kaiser and Rasminsky 1999, 21). In a more recent book the same authors give more detailed suggestions and prescriptions for preventing challenging behaviors, especially in relation to children's social context (Kaiser and Rasminsky 2003).

Lilian Katz and Diane McClellan, as they describe the importance of the teacher's role in *Fostering Children's Social Competence: The Teacher's Role,* write that "teachers can play a significant role in supporting social development. . . . What works well with young children is individualized guidance. . . . Individual focus and the warmth of the interaction increase the child's capacity to hear and respond deeply to the teacher's suggestions" (Katz and McClellan 1997, 19–20). Supported by a growing body of research, they warn that if teachers do not help children develop social competence, these children are likely to fail academically, drop out of school, or develop mental health problems. Throughout the book, the authors give teachers many different suggestions for helping children develop and learn social competency, including expressing respect for children's feelings, establishing authority and credibility, accommodating individual differences, encouraging impulse control, invoking ground rules, and so on (Katz and McClellan 1997, 66–72).

In addition to the books I've discussed above, I recommend that you take a look at the references at the end of this chapter. Many of these excellent books and articles about behavior management and effective social-emotional skills offer teachers helpful suggestions and strategies. In fact, in a later chapter I discuss a survey about teachers and anger that reveals that teachers certainly seem to have benefited from workshops, trainings, and books like these. At least they are able to describe word for word what they *should* be doing to help children with challenging behaviors. While I am sure that I have not exhausted the literature on this topic, most of the books and articles I have explored give interesting and helpful tips, prescriptions, steps, guidelines, suggestions, and descriptions of what to do to prevent and manage children's challenging behaviors. Nevertheless, I have not yet found one book or article that focuses specifically on assisting the adults who care for and educate young children to understand their personal feelings or emotional development in relation to these behaviors. Neither have I found a resource that makes connections between how teachers' emotions affect their interactions with children and families.

CONCLUSION

Back in 1954, more than forty years before the recent growing body of research about brain development, some teacher educators were concerned about preparing teachers to understand themselves through self-reflection. In an article titled "Understanding Others through Facing Ourselves," Arthur T. Jersild, a professor of education at Teachers College, Columbia University, in New York, suggested that "knowledge of self requires a different kind of personal involvement than the usual academic course encourages or demands" (Jersild 1954). According to Jersild, in order to acquire self-knowledge, "one must have the courage to seek it and the humility to accept what one may find."

66 Everything that enters into the relationship between a teacher and the child has or might have a significant bearing on what a child thinks about himself and how he feels about himself. Everything that transpires in a teacher's dealings with a child might also help the teacher to learn something about himself for his functioning as a teacher is to a large extent a projection of what he is.

In order to have insight into the child's strivings and the problems and issues he is coping with the teacher must strive to face the same issues within his own life. These issues are largely emotional in nature and the endeavor to understand oneself and others has a deep emotional meaning. It calls for more than intellectual cleverness and academic competence. 99 (Jersild 1954, 411)

Surely, we cannot think that teachers deal only with subject content like mathematics, literacy, or social studies and do not have to handle intense, emotional situations with young children moment by moment, day to day. If we agree that there is much personal and intimate involvement with children's expressions of feelings and their behaviors that constantly challenge us, then surely it is our moral and ethical responsibility to support teachers' self-reflection and awareness of their own emotions. Not to do so is a shirking of our responsibility as advocates of quality care and education for young children.

References

Gartrell, D. 2004. *The power of guidance: Teaching social-emotional skills in early childhood classrooms.* Clifton Park, N.Y.: Delmar Learning.

Gerhardt, S. 2004. *Why love matters: How affection shapes a baby's brain.* Hove, East Sussex: Brunner-Routledge.

Hammer, M. D. 2002. Beginnings workshop: "I'm bery, bery cwoss!" Understanding children's anger. *Child Care Information Exchange* (July): 38–41.

Howes, C., and S. Ritchie. 2002. *A matter of trust: Connecting teachers and learners in the early childhood classroom.* New York: Teachers College Press.

Hyson, M. 2002. Professional development: Emotional development and school readiness. *Young Children* 57 (6): 76–78.

———. 2004. *The emotional development of young children: Building an emotion-centered curriculum.* New York: Teachers College Press.

Jacobson, T. 2003. *Confronting our discomfort: Clearing the way for anti-bias in early childhood.* Portsmouth, N.H.: Heineman.

———. 2006. Resiliency in children: What we do matters. In *Child development: A beginnings workshop book*, ed. Bonnie Neugebauer. Redmond, Wash.: Exchange Press.

———. 2007. Book Review: *Unsmiling faces: Preschools that heal*, ed. Leslie Koplow, Teachers College Press. *Teachers College Record*, August 31, http://www.tcrecord.org.

Jersild, A. T. 1954. Understanding others through facing ourselves. *Childhood Education* (May): 411–14.

Kaiser, B., and J. S. Rasminsky. 1999. *Meeting the challenge: Effective strategies for challenging behaviours in early childhood environments.* Ottawa: Canadian Child Care Federation.

———. 2003. *Challenging behavior in young children: Understanding, preventing, and responding effectively.* Upper Saddle River, N.J.: Allyn and Bacon.

Karr-Morse, R., and M. S. Wiley. 1997. *Ghosts from the nursery: Tracing the roots of violence.* New York: Atlantic Monthly Press.

Katz, L. G., and D. E. McClellan. 1997. *Fostering children's social competence: The teacher's role.* Washington, D.C.: National Association for the Education of Young Children.

Koplow, L., ed. 2007. *Unsmiling faces: How preschools can heal.* New York: Teachers College Press.

Perry, B. D. 2007. *Early childhood and brain development: How experience shapes child, community and culture.* DVD. ChildTrauma Academy.

Perry, B. D., and M. Szalavitz. 2006. *The boy who was raised as a dog and other stories from a child psychiatrist's notebook: What traumatized children can teach us about loss, love, and healing.* New York: Basic Books.

Riley, D., R. R. San Juan, J. Klinkner, and A. Ramminger. 2008. *Social and emotional Development: Connecting science and practice in early childhood settings.* St. Paul: Redleaf Press.

Suggested Reading

Ahn, H. J. 2005. Child care teachers' strategies in children's socialization of emotion. *Early Childhood Development and Care* 175 (1): 49–61.

Baker, A. C., and L. A. Manfredi-Petitt. 2004. *Relationships, the heart of quality care: Creating community among adults in early care settings.* Washington, D.C.: National Association for the Education of Young Children.

Bronson, M. B. 2000. Recognizing and supporting the development of self-regulation in young children. *Young Children* 55 (2): 32–37.

Flicker, E. S., and J. A. Hoffman. 2002. Developmental discipline in the early childhood classroom. *Young Children* 57 (4): 82–89.

Katz, L. 1993. *Distinctions between self-esteem and narcissism: Implications for practice.* Urbana, Ill.: ERIC Clearinghouse on Early Education and Parenting.

Kontos, S., and A. Wilcox-Herzog. 1997. Research in review: Teachers' interactions with children: Why are they so important? *Young Children* 52 (2): 4–12.

———. 2002. Teacher preparation and teacher-child interaction in preschools. *ERIC Digest* (October): EDO-PS-02-11.

Lake, V. E. 2003. Practice in teaching should be practice in caring: Fidelity in teacher education. *Journal of Early Childhood Teacher Education* 24 (1): 73–81.

Lally, J. R. 1998. Beginnings workshop: Brain research, infant learning, and child care curriculum. *Child Care Information Exchange* (May): 46–48.

Marion, M. 1997a. Helping young children deal with anger. *ERIC Digest* (December): EDO-PS-97-24.

———. 1997b. Research in review: Guiding young children's understanding and management of anger. *Young Children* 57 (7): 62–67.

Moss, W. L. 2004. *Children don't come with an instruction manual: A teacher's guide to problems that affect learners.* New York: Teachers College Press.

Perry, B. D. 1997. Incubated in terror: Neurodevelopmental factors in the "cycle of violence." In *Children in a violent society*, ed. J. D. Osofsky. New York: Guilford Press.

Perry, B. D. 2007. *Early childhood and brain development: How experience shapes child, community, and culture.* DVD. ChildTrauma Academy.

Reinsberg, J. 1999. Understanding young children's behavior. *Young Children* 54 (4): 54–57.

Riley, D., R. R. San Juan, J. Klinkner, and A. Ramminger. 2008. *Social and emotional development: Connecting science and practice in early childhood settings.* St. Paul: Redleaf Press.

Rogovin, P. 2004. *Why can't you behave? The teacher's guide to creative classroom management, K–3.* Portsmouth, N.H.: Heinemann.

Stephens, K. 1996. Responding professionally and compassionately to challenging behavior. *Child Care Information Exchange* (September): 44–48.

Teicher, M. H. 2002. Scars that won't heal: The neurobiology of child abuse. *Scientific American* 286 (3): 68–75.

Vance, E., and P. J. Weaver. 2002. *Class meetings: Young children solving problems together.* Washington, D.C.: National Association for the Education of Young Children.

Wittmer, D. S., and A. S. Honig. 1994. Encouraging positive social development in young children. *Young Children* 49 (5): 4–12.

Your child: Birth to three. 2000. *Newsweek* special 2000 edition (fall and winter).

Zins, J. E. 2004. *Building academic success on social and emotional learning: What does the research say?* New York: Teachers College Press.

CHAPTER TWO

WE UNDERSTAND HOW
WE FEEL AND WHY

*Emotion matters are difficult, dense, subjective, personal,
communal, socially lived and understood, historical and
cultural, impossible to avoid, intertwined with all that we
say, think, write, know, withhold, remember, and wish to
forget. Emotion matters drive motives for action, speech,
judgment, and decision-making. . . . Emotion forms part of
how we come to develop attachments to others as well as
to objects and ideas. Emotion matters to teachers because
the classroom is alive with bodies, hearts, and selves, and
because learning is joyous, exciting, frightening, risky, passionate, boring, disappointing, and enraging. Emotion matters are inscribed in the teaching situation, a point too often
forgotten.*

—Laura R. Micciche

*It is an act of courage to acknowledge our own uncertainty
and sit with it for awhile.*

—Harriet Lerner

*There is courage in being accountable. We truly accept
responsibility for our own less-than-honorable behaviors,
even when doing so challenges our favored image of the
self.*

—Harriet Lerner

The Weirdest Class

A couple of years ago, at a college near Philadelphia, during the
last class of the semester, one of the undergraduate students gave
her presentation. As she was speaking, she began to cough. Her
face was turning red with embarrassment and her discomfort from
coughing—especially as she tried to suppress it. I offered her a sip
of water from my water bottle. She drank and then continued with
the presentation. However, the coughing continued, along with her
attempts to suppress it.

Finally, I interrupted the student by telling the class that many
years before, while living in Israel, I had taken a course in bioenergetics. I said that I did not have the time to tell them all the
details—just that it had something to do with storing emotions in
different energy points of the body and learning how to release the
energies through specific physical exercises. I explained how our

teacher, Rafi Rozen, had taught us that if, for example, we start coughing, we should probably cough and cough until we can cough no more. Just get it out! Everyone was listening to me while I talk-ed. The student continued to cough.

When I was done, a young woman in the class called out to the presenter, "Would you like us to cough with you?" I was surprised and glanced around at the students to see who had said that. They were all looking directly and intently at the student presenting and did not even seem to notice me looking about the room. Quickly, so as not to lose the moment, I said, "Let's all cough together." We all started coughing. Our presenter was coughing and smiling. She ex-claimed, "This is the weirdest class I have ever had." She turned to me with red cheeks, her coughing becoming faint, "I mean it's the best class. But it's so weird." I smiled and looked down for a mo-ment. It felt weird to me too. I had never done this before, at least not with adults.

I remembered that once, when I was a teacher in Israel many years before, I had stopped a circle time in midstream for a pre-schooler in my class. In the middle of my telling a story, a little girl stood up out of her chair and started screaming for what seemed to be no apparent reason. From time to time she would do that and always, it seemed, at circle time. We had tried everything. The as-sistant had taken her out of the room to calm her down, and we had even asked her parents for more information. They told us they had not seen her do it at home. On this particular day, not knowing how to handle the situation and without thinking too much about it, I said to the class (in Hebrew), "Wow! It looks like Karen just needs to scream. Let's sit and listen with her." We all sat quietly while the child stood and continued to scream at the top of her lungs. One of the children put his hands over his ears and screwed up his brow. Another said, "Let's bring her some water to drink." Yet another called out, "She needs a tissue." I encouraged the two children who had spoken up to bring a glass of water and some tissues. After a few moments they returned. The little girl stopped screaming. She stared at the two children bearing gifts. She blew her nose, drank some water, and then sat back down in her chair. The room became still for a moment. Without further comment, I continued to read the story.

It had not seemed "weird" at the time, all those years ago, to support one of the four-year-olds having difficulties while I was reading a story. The story could wait. It did not even matter really why she was screaming. It seemed more important that our small community should just listen and be there for her, for whatever the reason. Come to think of it, I was probably influenced by the few times people listened to me and were not afraid of me when I had cried or shared my pain as a child. Those memories are still clear to me, memories of kindness and compassion. They guide me through those emotional-situation moments when I simply do not know what to do with a child's behavior that I consider challenging.

I looked up out of my brief reverie, my memory of when I was a teacher of young children. I wondered why it was weird taking the same approach with my adult learners. A few minutes later the undergraduate student said, "Okay, I feel better now." She had stopped coughing. She completed her presentation. Everyone applauded. For a moment, I felt a sort of community energy in the room, the type of feeling that comes when a group of people have prayed or meditated together.

OUR OWN EMOTIONAL DEVELOPMENT HAS AN IMPACT ON HOW WE DEAL WITH CHILDREN.

Confronting Our Emotions

Children have no problem showing us they are confused and frightened by feelings they cannot control or explain. Indeed, some of their reactions are intense and downright noisy. When we are faced with children's emotions, we are tested with our responses time and again. Sometimes we are at a loss about what to do, just like with my little four-year-old, Karen, who would scream when I read a story at circle time. Often we are faced with memories of ways we were handled when we were children, and these past experiences are liable to cloud our judgment even when we are knowledgeable about child development and appropriate practice. Dealing with emotions is just too emotional!

We are all striving to be the best teachers we can be. Each one of us defines that differently. One of the exercises I give students at the beginning of their student teaching experience is to answer this question: What does it mean for you to be the best teacher you can be? Their answers vary:

> to reach out and help children succeed academically
>
> to understand that everyone is different and not force children to become someone they are not
>
> to be caring, understanding, and trustworthy
>
> to be a role model and someone for children to look up to
>
> to be a supplier of knowledge and information

to be an effective communicator and understand that
people have different learning styles

to be inspirational and sensitive

to create a trusting, emotional, and intellectual environment
so that children are less apprehensive about learning

to be respectful, kind, fair, and considerate

to be able to discuss life problems openly "

As they start out in their teaching career, new teachers are full
of passion and wonder about the profession. Many of them talk
about creating emotionally safe classrooms for their students.

From the beginning of my career as a teacher I always wanted
to give children a safe emotional environment. There they would
be accepted unconditionally, their feelings would be validated, and
all would be supported in becoming the best they could be. As I
have had multiple opportunities for self-reflection, I know today
that I wanted to give children what I never had. In fact, the more
I worked at providing emotional safety for children, the more I
learned about my own childhood and what had been lacking, what
had been comforting, and what had hurt me growing up. Indeed,
working with young children was often therapeutic for me. I was
able to understand why I feel what I feel and how I do what I do
in relation to those feelings. It was not always comfortable to face
some of these feelings. It was more often than not uncomfortable
and disconcerting. I would find myself after school, sitting quietly
to write or think about what had been so disturbing for me with
this or that child during the day.

Even with all our best intentions, our passionate efforts to
be the best teachers we can be, we are often confronted with

discomfort in regard to our own feelings. Some of us even start to experience burnout when we are constantly faced with children flailing about in emotional situations and find that we are at a loss about how to help them.

Most of the time we are not even aware that our own feelings are in the way of resolving an emotionally charged situation with some of our youngest children. Confronting emotions is not an easy task. Some of us do not allow ourselves to be aware of what we are feeling. For example, it took years for me to discover that when I am afraid, ashamed, angry, confused, or worried, I tend to giggle a little when I speak. In other words, my giggle is sometimes a warning sign for me to alert myself that I am becoming uncomfortable. For others, though, it can be confusing. They are not sure whether to take me seriously or not. So I might say, "I don't like it when you do thus and such," but at the same time I am conveying a mixed message because I am smiling and softly laughing a little uneasily as I speak. When trying to set a clear and consistent boundary for young children, mixed messages are seldom helpful.

A few years ago I facilitated a support-supervision group for early childhood professionals working on their attitudes of bias. During one of the sessions a preschool teacher shared with the group how one of the boys in her class was a challenge (Jacobson 2003). In short, she did not like him and did not know how to handle his angry outbursts. She described how she did not even like to look at him sometimes. During the next couple of weeks we probed further and discussed her feelings about that specific child. As she uncovered her own earlier personal memories of her life, she realized that the boy reminded her of an ex-lover and a difficult relationship in her past. As the weeks went by, she described how her discomfort with his anger had decreased since she had been able to connect to her own feelings. In the final group session she excitedly disclosed that the child had expressed disappointment about her anticipated move from his class to another within the center:

" Remember the struggle I had about that thing with the angry stuff I had with him? By working through it here [the support group], some of it, I was able to then work with him in a different way . . . and I was saying that when he found out that I wasn't gonna be the teacher in the room any more, he was jumping up and down, literally jumping up and down going, "No, you can't go! No, you can't go!" I looked at him and said, "T.H. is that you?" I couldn't believe it. Obviously we'd gotten somewhere because he would never have done that, I don't think. " (Jacobson 2003, 101)

Anger is only one of the many feelings we experience when working with young children. Children are bundles of emotion as they explore their world, observing the significant adults in their lives and learning what is acceptable and expected of them in becoming citizens of their culture and society. Love, joy, disappointment, jealousy, shame, guilt, ecstasy, desire, fear—these are just a few of the emotions we all have learned to feel, express, or repress in one way or another. Human beings are complex and diverse in how we learn to deal with feelings, starting in our families of origin and expanding into the society at large.

My father-in-law once heard Garrison Keillor, the popular radio show host, mention that Scandinavians are suspicious of intensity. My father-in-law especially enjoyed that comment, even though he realized it was a generalization and a stereotype, because he himself is of Norwegian descent and was taught to remain calm, cool, and collected in the face of fear, anger, and even exuberance or ecstasy. In fact, he was taught to be suspicious of intensity. The ways in which we are taught to express our feelings are often influenced by cultural or societal norms or mores and not only by family members who love and care for us.

Leaving Our Personal Lives at the Door

I have always been impressed with teachers who tell me that they are capable of leaving their personal lives at the door. In other words, no matter what is bothering them or making them anxious at home, they are able to put those worries aside and focus only on the children in the classroom. I must admit that I am capable of doing this. In fact, sometimes it is helpful, even comforting, to stop thinking troubling thoughts and concentrate only on the immediate work at hand. When student interns are having difficulties with their cooperating teachers, they come to me for advice, especially when the situation seems to get in the way of their working effectively with the children. Sometimes we are able to resolve their issues quite quickly. At other times it looks as if they are going to have to work with the cooperating teacher even when the relationship is not conducive to learning the best possible practices. When that happens, I tell the students to "pour themselves into the children." By that I mean that I want them to focus on getting to know the children—their needs, the ways they learn, and how to relate to them—rather than allowing personal or professional problems to become obstacles.

This type of professional focus is essential to our work with children. It is important to be present and available to others who need us in the many small and major interactions in the classroom. As focused as we may think we are, however, our emotional shadows find a way to haunt us when we least expect them. We are not always able to put our finger on which feeling in particular we are experiencing or why we are suddenly uncomfortable. It could be in the way we uncontrollably blurt out a sentence and discover to our surprise that we sound exactly like our mother, father, aunt, grandmother, or cousin. Or it might manifest itself in sweating, trembling, stomach problems, or headaches. For example, one of my students described to the class recently that when the door of her dormitory room starts to open as a friend walks in, she finds herself becoming anxious and feels a tightening in her throat. She recalled that her mother used to come into her room when she was a child and yell at her, calling her names and frightening her. And so now, as an adult, she experiences general anxiety whenever any-one comes into her room.

These types of anxieties might unconsciously affect how we re-act. It becomes difficult for us to leave our personal life at the door if we do not take the time to understand how early childhood experiences influence our responses.

A Note about Anger

One morning I made myself a great fruit shake: apple, orange, ba-nana, pear, blueberries, pine nuts, raspberries, dates, grapes, half a cup of soy milk, and half a cup of freshly squeezed orange juice—all blended up into a smooth delicious shake. Usually a full glass of fruit shake like that fills me up for half a day. On that day, however, after half an hour I was ravenous! I prowled the kitchen moaning and rumbling, "Food, food, food." I muttered, "I need breakfast." My husband suggested an omelet and turkey sausage, toast, and tomato. "Yum!" I replied, licking my lips, beginning to salivate. Out came all the ingredients as my partner in life proceeded to prepare the meal. I wandered into the living room as the pots and pans, plates and forks clattered and clanged. I stood facing the large window looking out onto Fairmount Park, admiring the blooming forsythia and budding trees. I murmured to myself, "Maybe this will quell my *anger* finally." I spun around, surprised as if hearing a loud noise. "I mean *hunger* not *anger*," I said out loud. My husband looked up quizzically from his cooking, not quite understanding what was going on out there—in my own mind. What a slip of the tongue! I realized that my hunger had something to do with feeling angry. I had not been aware of any anger at that moment, and yet the words slipped out of my mouth smoothly, clearly, assuredly.

Indeed, I had been feeling quite angry that week. A few things had been happening, as they do in life, and always when I leave a place I have become slightly attached to I feel angry. Separation is not easy for me. Making a stand is not comfortable for me either. I had been doing quite a bit of both at that time. In class the week before I had noticed that I was feeling uncomfortable and agitated. My tone was sharp, and some of my comments to my students were harsh and sarcastic. Midway through the session, I asked the students if they had noticed my anger. Some of them nodded their heads up and down vehemently. Others said, "Yes!" emphatically. Even as I was feeling quite bewildered, I shared my reflective process out loud, trying to understand what was happening to me: "I think because I was away all week it feels like I've lost you. I sense a need to bring you all back under my wing. Also, my leaving the college is affecting me. I think I am feeling angry because of all these things. If I have said anything to hurt any of you today, I am truly sorry." Then I sighed deeply, and the tension in the room eased. Some students smiled and seemed to shift in their seats to more comfortable positions. The next day I received an e-mail from one of them:

" I really appreciate your honesty, your willingness to be vulnerable. . . . When you admitted last week that you were
feeling angry . . . and modeled for us how to find out why
we are angry—that was awesome. That taught me so much.
I think sometimes people think they are the only person
who feels certain things. What you demonstrated showed
all of us that you are human, you have feelings, you feel
angry, hurt, etc. I think we need more professors, teachers,
caregivers who are honest. "

What a teachable moment! Who would have thought? I certainly never planned that one. It was one of those spontaneous, unin-
tentional moments that worked. It occurred to me that during that
week I had been thinking a lot about anger consciously just as it
was developing unconsciously. It was no coincidence, for I had been
conducting a survey about teachers and anger for the six weeks pri-
or—gathering data for a chapter, perhaps, in this very book, where
I am exploring how teachers' emotions affect their interactions with
children, especially when there are challenging behaviors.

When I think, talk, or write about teachers' emotions in general, anger becomes a large—indeed huge—topic that deserves a
chapter all on its own. Anger: that complex, necessary emotion
we all experience from time to time. Very few embrace feeling angry; most of us fear it or hate it, do not know what to do, deny
or ignore it. Some say they never feel it at all. So many women I
know get headaches or cry when they are feeling angry, and heaven
knows, I've just realized that I become hungry! It seems to me
that when children are angry, it makes us feel helpless, vulnerable,
afraid, uncomfortable, and out of control. Children's anger immediately becomes something adults need to quell, quash, repress,

redirect, close down, shut out, punish, or get rid of. Holding still and helping a child explore and process all those tumultuous, complicated feelings is seldom considered an option. And yet we all so desperately need to find ways to express our anger productively in order to make a stand for who we are and what we believe in. If adults cannot help children do this, who will? So here I am, my personal feelings affecting my professional life. The more I explore the relationship between anger and teaching, the more I become aware of my own anger. And there it is, staring right back at me as I interact with students or associated with a sudden hunger just after I have eaten a nourishing meal.

ACTIONS TO TAKE

Take note of how you respond to the following questions:

- Does too much expression of enthusiasm or joyousness make you feel overwhelmed or uneasy?
- Do you find that you tend to calm children down when they exclaim loudly with glee or engage exuberantly in rough and tumble play with each other?
- Do you enjoy children bounding up to you to hug or climb onto you? Or do you find that you pull back, afraid of an intrusion into your personal physical space?

Think about Your Response to Boisterousness

Once, one of my colleagues called me with a sense of urgency to come to the one-way mirrored observation window of the small laboratory school at the graduate college where I was assistant director. She was concerned that our new male teacher was playing rough and tumble games with a group of preschoolers. As I stood at the observation window watching the teacher playing with the children, who squealed with delight, I suddenly heard the words of my own mother echoing through the chambers of my memory: "Be careful—this will end in tears!" I shared this reflection with my colleague, and we discussed why we felt uncomfortable. Was it really inappropriate and dangerous for the teacher to be playing with the children in that manner? Or was this more about feeling uncomfortable because we had been taught to be cautious about exuberance when we were children? In the end, we concluded that it was our own discomfort that was getting in the way of understanding those young children's need for rough and tumble play.

How do you feel about children's noisiness? When I was a validator for the National Association for the Education of Young Children (NAEYC) accreditation system some years ago, one of the criteria of an appropriate early childhood program used to be that teachers' voices should not dominate, and that children were observed to be busy talking and interacting with one another. Indeed, children's voices in my classrooms could always be heard way above and beyond those of the teachers as they played and worked with one another throughout their learning centers. Recently, I was invited by the superintendent of our local school district to tour a couple of elementary schools. When we walked through the first one, I noticed that the school was quiet—so quiet, in fact, that I became anxious. I asked my hosts, "How come the children are so quiet? What have you done to them?" Everyone laughed, and the principal explained that they were busy at work, learning, in the classrooms. As we entered the second school of my guided tour, I immediately heard the sounds of children's voices. Classroom doors were propped open, parents were visiting, and children were coming and going to restrooms or to the gym for choir practice in preparation for an upcoming holiday concert. I must have looked happy about the raised level of children's voices, because the assistant to the superintendent noted quietly, "Here we can hear the children. I think you like that." I smiled at her and nodded my head vehemently. "I love the sound of children," I replied. Some principals allow the noisiness of children to prevail. Others prefer children to be very, very quiet.

When I was the director of a large university child care center, I once had a new infant teacher come and complain to me. She was appalled by the way we allowed the older infants to scream or squeal while they were eating lunch. I explained that at that age children were experimenting with their voices, learning sounds and ways to express themselves. She said that children must be quiet when they eat, and she would resign unless we changed that policy. Needless to say, I regretfully accepted her resignation.

Think about Shame and Fear

Intense feelings like shame or fear affect us in many different ways. Lerner calls fear, anxiety, and shame the "big three" of emotions (Lerner 2004). No one is immune to them. These emotions are particularly present when we are faced with hardship or tragedy. As many of us continue teaching through good and bad times, we are bound to be caught up in one or all of these emotions at one time or another while we work and interact with young children or with students. While fear is an emotion that is sometimes necessary to warn us of danger, Lerner suggests that we might consider decoding it for different, more unconscious messages. She asks:

" Are we feeling anxious because we are boldly charting new
territory, or because we're about to do something stupid?
Sometimes we feel a stab of fear . . . because our unconscious is warning us that we're truly off track. . . . Perhaps
we shouldn't rush into a particular job, conversation, trip,
marriage, or divorce. In such cases, fear can operate as a
wise protector, one we need to honor and respect. Yet if
fear was always a legitimate warning signal, we might never
show up for a doctor's appointment, speak up when we feel
passionate about something, or leave a dead-end relationship. There are times when we need to push past our dread
and resolve—with our hearts pounding in our chests—to
act. " (Lerner 2004, 5)

According to Lerner, shame, on the other hand, often lies below our
fears, and we rarely talk about it. Indeed, we might even keep our
shame a secret from ourselves. We are ashamed of our shame! It is
a social emotion because we usually feel shame in front of someone
else. This is the part of ourselves that we consider flawed and that
should not be seen by others, whether it is something physical (like
a part of our bodies), or the part of our psyche that is too weak or
too loud or

" . . . the part that wants to dazzle and shine and be the center of attention, the part that takes up "too much" space—
or not enough. Shame drives the fear of not being good
enough. . . . You can learn to feel shame about anything
that is real about you—your shape, your accent, your finan-
cial situation, your wrinkles, your size, your illness, your
infertility, how you spend your day. " (Lerner 2004, 118)

It is important to mention that guilt feels similar to shame. It accompanies and guides us in our work with children, students, and families. However, whereas shame is connected to who we feel we are, guilt is usually linked to our behaviors, beliefs, or values. Lerner makes a distinction between the two: "Guilt is about *doing*. Shame is about *being*" (Lerner 2004, 121). I think of the difference this way: If I behave inappropriately with a child in my care, and feel a healthy guilt about it, I am able to choose different ways of behaving the next time. If I experience shame, I am liable to become debilitated and paralyzed to act because all I feel is what a bad person I am.

When I was in my first year of teaching young children, I would become alarmed and frightened when a child would act in a way that some call "throwing a tantrum." The child's body stiffened, screams were loud and uncontrollable, and sometimes the child threw things or kicked and spat at me. At first I felt fear because I did not know how to respond. And then I felt shame because I would feel helpless and, thus, a failure. It seemed as if the children and my teacher aide would look to me to resolve this issue. Even the image I had of myself as a teacher was shattered in the face of an imaginary audience I created in my own mind. I was found out from within myself! I was a fraud and should obviously not be teaching if I was clearly so incompetent.

The older and more experienced I became, the more I was able to put aside these debilitating images of myself and focus directly on what emotionally confused and distraught children clearly needed from me: boundaries to keep them (and the others around them) safe, understanding, validation, respect for their feelings, and emotional support. As long as I was wrapped up in my own shame and fear, I was powerless to help them. Shame is one of those emotions that accompany us when we act inappropriately even while knowing how or what we should really be doing.

In the following chapter I expand the discussion about facing our emotions and take a longer, more in-depth look at anger specifically. This emotion is not always handled in a way that is helpful either to adults or to children. I say this based on my experiences as a former teacher of young children and as a teacher educator who visits diverse early childhood programs in many different states. I have always feared acknowledging and expressing my anger, thinking that it is a bad or shameful emotion. It has taken me almost all my life to realize that anger is a productive and useful emotion that, if acknowledged and understood, will guide me into taking care of my needs as well as protecting the rights of others. Indeed, I am unable to understand reasons for my anger or thus express it effectively if I am afraid or ashamed of it. Therefore, the issue is not the anger per se. Rather, it is how to express it effectively.

CONCLUSION

Human beings are complex and interesting, with intense emotions that can protect and guide us as well as block and confuse us. All of us feel some sort of emotion all of the time. Anger, shame, fear, guilt, joy, sorrow, hate, love, disappointment, jealousy, regret, embarrassment, anxiety, happiness, contentment, satisfaction, elation, humility, pride . . . I could go on and on and still not cover all the types of emotions human beings experience. Perhaps you can think of some that I have left out or forgotten here? No matter what the emotions are, as early childhood educators, we have a responsibility to identify which of *our* emotions—those that are unconscious or ones we are aware of—affect our interactions with children and their families.

References

Jacobson, T. 2003. *Confronting our discomfort: Clearing the way for anti-bias in early childhood*. Portsmouth, N.H.: Heinemann.

Lerner, H. 2004. *The dance of fear: Rising above anxiety, fear, and shame to be your best and bravest self*. New York: HarperCollins.

Lerner, H. G. 1985. *The dance of anger: A woman's guide to changing the patterns of intimate relationships*. New York: Harper and Row.

Micciche, L. R. 2007. *Doing emotion: Rhetoric, writing, teaching*. Portsmouth, N.Y.: Boynton Cook.

CHAPTER THREE

WE UNDERSTAND THE
POWER OF OUR ANGER

*I especially liked the approach because I sensed my own an-
ger at Steven as he continued to monopolize so much of my
time, and these positive techniques helped me cover up my
negative feelings. But it was not working. His moments of
extreme hostility seemed to be increasing. What was I doing
wrong? Did he sense my anger?*

—VIVIAN GUSSIN PALEY

*To be able to sympathize with the child who is hostile . . .
the teacher must face his own hostile tendencies and try to
accept the implication of his anger as it occurs, say, in his
annoyance with his pupils, his impatience with himself, his
feuds with other teachers, his complaints against parents or*

*school authorities or others on whom he fixes his ire. The
more a person can face some of the ramifications of his own
anger and make some allowance for his tendency to become
angry, the more sensitive he can be to the hurts, frustrations, and anxieties involved in another person's anger.*

—ARTHUR T. JERSILD

Some of you may have read *The Dance of Anger* by Harriet Lerner.
I reached for it again recently because during a past illness I experienced quite a bit of anger—constant niggling, simmering anger
at my body "giving in." It rendered me helpless and exhausted, especially because I mostly internalized it into a mild kind of depres-
sion. My anger was, in fact, debilitating. Although I did not express
it outwardly, I was seething within. As I was rereading Lerner,
thinking that I needed to brush up on information about women
and anger for this book, I came upon a sentence that seemed to fit
my particular situation: "Fighting and blaming is sometimes a way
both to protest and to protect the status quo when we are not quite
ready to make a move in one direction or another" (Lerner 1985,
33). I stopped dead in my tracks.

All that simmering, seething anger (internal, silent fighting and
blaming of my health and circumstances) was debilitating indeed.
But it was serving me well, as it held me down and in place. Not
only was I ill, but I was feeling helpless and frustrated at the same
time. The day after I had been reading and thinking about the
source of my anger, I awoke much clearer than on any of the days
of the two prior weeks. The illness really felt as if it was finally dis-
sipating, and I seemed less afraid and helpless. This was not a big
deal revelation or anything—just a reminder. Anger will always
come and go. Sometimes I will allow it to hold me down and in

place emotionally and even physically, it seems. And, at times, I will recognize it for the helpful warning sign it is.

THE COMPLEXITY OF ANGER MEANS WE MUST ADDRESS IT CAREFULLY AND THOROUGHLY.

Anger, Adults, and Children

One of the most intense emotions that we all experience while guiding young children's behaviors is anger—children's as well as our own. Young children have different, more open and volatile ways of expressing anger: punching, kicking, throwing things, spitting, scratching, screaming, biting—to name a few. As adults, we are not proud of the emotion of anger. Nor do we seem willing to talk about it very much. Many people choose to euphemize it by calling anger anything but its real name, using words like "frustration" or "discomfort." For example, one of my colleagues uses the term "interesting" in place of any intense emotion she is describing. This reminds me of people who are ashamed to admit that they *hate* something or someone. Instead, they use the word "dislike" to soften the intensity or reality of the emotion. While most pre-service teachers describe a scripted acceptance of anger—for example, "we need to help children express their anger appropriately," or "anger is a useful emotion because it tells us that our rights are being violated and we have a right to our feelings"—at the same time, they share fear or anxiety when it comes to expressing or even acknowledging their own anger. Each semester I ask students who are learning to be early childhood teachers what they learned about expressing anger when they were young children. Time and again they tell me that anger is a bad emotion, could be dangerous, and needs to be suppressed or "gotten rid of." They describe feeling extreme frustration or as if they might lose control—or even become crazy.

Haven't we all been angry at one time or another in our lives? Life is not always easy or fun when we are growing up. When we were children, adults did not always allow us to do whatever we wanted, and many times we were disciplined for things we thought we did not do. Sometimes our parents' decisions seemed unfair, or we did not understand the reason for their reactions to us. Often our parents were unpredictable or became upset with things we said, and they did not always explain clearly enough their reasons or emotional reactions to our behaviors. Growing up we learned to navigate the emotional climate of family members. Then, later, we were faced with new challenges in school and society at large. We spent a lot of our childhood waiting our turn, standing in lines, learning to share, and developing skills for friendships and other relationships with others. It was not always easy, and many times we experienced feelings of anger, frustration, disappointment, jealousy, helplessness, and anxiety, to name a few.

When children express anger, it is sometimes alarming and even a little frightening for them. It can feel out of control or even a bit like they might be going crazy. Sometimes it feels like that for the adults around them as well. In fact, some teachers have told me that at times they are afraid of children who are angry. Adults try to get rid of the child's anger using different methods. They most likely learned some of those methods from the significant adults in their lives when they were growing up. They may say things like: "Be quiet. Stop it. It's not nice to say things like that." Or they might ignore the outburst and walk to the other side of room, pretending they do not see or hear the anger. At times, they might use various punishments to curb the child's expression, including giving the child a time-out, putting the child in a corner, shouting at the child or scolding, and even hitting or other forms of physical punishment.

Very early in life, all of us as children get the message that anger is not a good emotion. And the worst part about it is that anger keeps on returning. Try as we might to push it away, it comes back again! Each time we feel violated or threatened, anger rises up to greet us. In fact, anger is one of those emotions we need to help us survive. It assists us in getting our needs met. It protects us when things are amiss. Instead of ignoring or trying to get rid of anger, we could learn to recognize it, understand why we are feeling angry, and develop ways for this emotion to be useful or productive for us. But children cannot undergo this process alone. They need the significant adults in their lives to guide them in accepting anger as one of the many different emotions we experience as human beings. Anger is part of who we are. It is neither good nor bad. The way we learn to express it is crucial in helping us negotiate relationships with other human beings and become viable, responsible citizens of our communities. Learning to express anger productively makes us all safe.

Survey on Teachers and Anger

Anger is one of the most complex emotions for adults to deal with because of all the guilt and shame that is attached to it. Therefore, I created a survey (see the appendix) to explore further how early childhood professionals understand anger—their own and that of children in their classrooms. The survey was distributed to some three hundred participants at the National Coalition for Campus Children's Centers national conference in Denver (spring 2006) and to about fifty teachers in different early childhood programs in New Jersey (spring 2007). Surveys were mainly administered to early childhood classroom teachers, although about 25 percent were given to student teachers and some program administrators. One of the sampling considerations was that the survey was distributed mostly to national campus children's centers. These centers are sometimes considered higher quality than regular early childhood programs in the community because of their placement on university campuses. If this is the case, we might expect the teachers and caregivers in these types of settings to be better trained. The implication is that teachers in regular community programs are in even more need of support for this type of self-reflection. However, teachers from regular community programs in New Jersey responded in an identical manner. Some of the questions asked were *qualitative* in nature. For example:

- Please describe what anger feels like to you.
- What do you do when children express anger in your classroom?
- Please explain why it was okay or why it was not okay to express anger around your parents when you were a child.

Others were demographic questions: age, gender, length of time in the profession, cultural background, and educational qualifications. Preliminary analysis of the data included creating categories or themes that emerged from the qualitative questions and making connections, if any, between those and the demographic information. (For example: Do males and females experience anger differently? Or: Do different numbers of years of teaching experience suggest different types of reactions to children's anger?) Then I looked for implications for teacher education or future research.

Preliminary analysis of the survey information yielded one notable finding that is relevant to the discussion in this chapter. When asked how they experience anger themselves, participants in the survey uniformly describe anger in a negative way, with much emotional detail. Some examples include:

- When my inside[s] turn over into a knot. I want to yell and my ears turn hot! I also tend to get tears in my eyes!
- A buildup of strong emotions that makes me feel hot and often times causes me to cry.
- A feeling that I have no control over something that has happened that is upsetting to me.
- I can't think rationally, I feel my palms get sweaty. My knees start to shake, my voice cracks. I talk louder and faster; it makes me understand why shaken-baby syndrome happens. Not to condone it but I understand how a parent can get to that point.
- I feel I have to remove myself from the situation in order to avoid yelling. It makes me feel frustrated and helpless.
- Anger feels hot. Red hot. Sometimes it comes at you like a tidal wave. Sometimes it builds and builds until it turns into a volcano and explodes.
- Anger feels like you want to explode and just scream or hit something. It makes you hot and uncomfortable and anxious.

In addition, participants in the survey describe how children make them angry. Some examples include:

- When a child doesn't listen to what I am or other children are saying to them. Also when they have been asked over and over to work on something and the child doesn't respond or follow through with the task.

- Children who know the rules and don't follow them.
- Children using their hands instead of their words—most importantly—children being mean to others (teasing/name calling). I have little tolerance for that.
- I find that when I am tired, sick, or frustrated about something else, I get angry more easily.
- I have gotten angry at children who have hurt another child or a child who repeatedly does something I have asked him not to do.
- I hate whining. Whining makes me very angry.
- When children say they don't need the bathroom, then five minutes later they do.
- Being ignored or provoked, being hit, spit on, called names.
- When children hurt other children or myself.
- When children do things on purpose to evoke a negative response.
- When children talk back or don't listen.

The vast majority—99 percent—of teachers in the survey said what you would want them to say with regard to how they *deal* with children and anger. Their answers to the question "What do you do when children express anger in your classroom?" are almost scripted, as if from some training manual or policy of the program or school in which they teach. Indeed, I imagine that many of these answers come from either the very publications in the reference list in chapter 1 of this book or behavior management workshops that teachers have attended. One thing seems obvious to me: at least teachers know what they are expected to say. Some examples include:

- I acknowledge their feelings and try to help them express their anger verbally.
- We allow them to be upset as long as they aren't hurting themselves or others. We give them a safe place to throw their fit.
- We tell them that it's okay to be upset or angry but that they need to walk away or sit down and have some private time to be upset so that they don't hurt their friends (if it's physical). If not physically acting out anger we like them to tell us or their friends why they are upset.
- We try not to stifle their emotions, but make sure they don't hurt themselves or others at the same time if applicable to the situation.
- Tell them it's okay to be angry but we cannot hurt people or destroy property when we are angry or ever.
- Ask them if they are angry. Have them tell a teacher or their friend if they are angry and why.
- Help the children problem solve when they are angry.

In fact, it appears as if the literature and staff development trainings about behavior management strategies and emotional development have worked! Teachers and administrators certainly know what to *say* about how they *should* manage children's behaviors, specifically with regard to anger. Their negative and sometimes volatile expressions about feeling angry themselves changed instantly to a type of professional script when it came to their ways of managing children's anger.

This finding—teachers saying one thing about anger in children but another about their own experience of anger—raises further questions. For example, do teachers follow these instructions out of duty or fear, or are they intrinsically aware of and/or motivated by them? In other words, how do these policies connect with teachers' belief systems or feelings about discipline in general? Second, is it true, in fact, that all teachers become calm and professional, in this scripted way, in their interactions with children? Do they actually act so professionally in their interactions with children who make them feel the anger they describe so readily in response to the qualitative question? Or are they answering the questions in a way that they assume the researcher, administrators, supervisors, or this author wants to hear?

My experience as a former preschool teacher and, presently, as a teacher educator observing teachers in the field is that teachers more often than not react quite differently from the script-like things they say in the survey when confronted with children's challenging behaviors. For example, two early childhood interns who studied with me in an early childhood practicum class reported that their cooperating teacher demonstrated aggressively angry behaviors with children she considered problematic. The teacher grabbed a child's arm, dragging her across the classroom and sitting her down in a harsh manner, while loudly scolding. This teacher was among those answering the survey with a professional script of acceptance about guiding children in a respectful manner.

According to Marilou Hyson, "Whatever their beliefs, all adults who work with young children become genuinely angry at times" (Hyson 2004). Further, she suggests it is helpful to identify which situations might be the cause of such feelings, and she acknowledges that "modeling the expression of anger is a complex, difficult task. Although conscientious teachers avoid deliberately frightening children with excessive displays of anger, it is not easy to maintain a balance between allowing children to experience a model of honest anger and overwhelming them with inappropriate, poorly controlled emotion" (Hyson 2004, 78, 79).

This type of say-one-thing-but-do-another phenomenon raises additional questions. What connections, if any, might be made between personal feelings and professional interactions? How do teachers deal with the conflict between the personal and the professional when these feelings do arise? In other words, I might understand what should be done and even agree with what I am reading or being told to do. But at times my personal emotions become too strong for the learned, professional script, and I find myself behaving in ways that are inappropriate. How does that make me feel? Guilty? Ashamed? Feelings of shame and guilt do not make us more competent or appropriate. They reinforce bad feelings about ourselves, which, in turn, could paralyze us or, worse still, make us behave even more inappropriately the next time. Finally, how can teacher educators, administrators, and supervisors support self-reflection about this issue specifically?

The almost identical, scripted statements about the acceptability of children's anger and ways to handle situations show that teachers in the survey are aware of what to say about appropriate interactions. But does it mean that they *do* what they say they believe? Whatever way teachers behave, they need support to help them understand why they do what they do when they are angry with children. This can help to prevent harsh caregiving or humiliating and disrespectful interactions with children.

Misplacing the Anger

It is important to remember that anger itself is neither bad nor shameful. The harm can come in how we express or repress it. Of course, this information may not sound new to you. We have learned by now that it is not good for our bodies or souls if we repress uncomfortable emotions for too long. Nor does it really benefit those around us, whether in personal or professional relationships. Anger seeps out in all sorts of ways: passively, aggressively, through illness and headaches, destructively, or explosively.

There is a lot to process when it comes to feeling angry. I have often heard it said that it is a good idea to stop and count to ten or three (or whatever number suits you) before reacting when enraged. As teachers, we must realize that it is more than just counting to ten. Reacting without thinking might give a child a message he will internalize for life! All too often it is easy to misplace our anger on the children around us. They are helpless and needy, and we have all the power. If we are feeling helpless and needy too, or have unresolved anger from childhood, it is our responsibility as educators to uncover the reasons why. We set the tone in our classrooms. It is our mood that creates the climate.

ACTIONS TO TAKE

Teachers and caregivers of young children have different reasons for and different types of experiences with anger. Some are directly related to children's behaviors. In other words, children can do things that make us angry. Often these feelings bring up conscious or unconscious memories about how we were treated as young children when expressing anger—whether we were permitted to express it, discouraged from expressing it, or disciplined when we expressed it. Our reactions are as varied as can be. Each of us had different life experiences unique to our personalities, our place in the family, how we were treated, and how we developed emotional memory, attachment, trust, and sense of self-worth.

What types of children's behaviors make you angry? Reflect on recent interactions or challenges, and make a list of the types of behaviors that cause you discomfort. Is it children talking back or questioning a given command, biting, hitting, spitting, pushing, taking things from other children, kicking, whining? Read the survey on anger in the appendix, especially the questions that ask how your family allowed you to express anger or how you describe yourself feeling angry. As you answer the questions, perhaps it will help to jog your memory about times you have felt angry in your personal life or in the classroom. For example, think about the ways you were disciplined when you were a child, especially for expressing anger. In a following chapter I will discuss further how we were affected when disciplined as young children.

CONCLUSION

"The most practical thing we can achieve in any kind of work is insight into what is happening inside us as we do it," writes Parker Palmer in *The Courage to Teach* (Palmer 1998, 5). According to Palmer:

> The entanglements I experience in the classroom are often no more or less than the convolutions of my inner life. Viewed from this angle, teaching holds a mirror to the soul.

If I am willing to look in that mirror and not run from what I see, I have a chance to gain self knowledge—and knowing myself is as crucial to good teaching as knowing my students and my subject. " (Palmer 1998, 2)

Chances are, if we are experiencing anger, there is an excellent reason for it: our rights are being violated, or an injustice occurred. The key is not to repress it but to allow ourselves to find a way to express it that is productive and beneficial. But first we might have to uncover the reasons why or how we came to feel this way. As Palmer suggests, it takes courage to hold still and face uncomfortable feelings.

Children learn a lot by our example. They learn to be open and honest if we are. And they learn to express anger productively if we are able to share that skill with them. All of the freedom movements in the world throughout the ages came about because people had simply had enough of their rights being violated. Some of them were successful in their expressions of outrage. Others were irresponsible and destructive. In the classroom, teachers are always the people with the power over young children and how they feel. And with an emotion as volatile as anger, our responsibility to understand and confront it is as awesome as can be.

References

Hyson, M. 2004. *The emotional development of young children: Building an emotion-centered curriculum.* 2nd ed. New York: Teachers College Press.

Jersild, A. T. 1954. Understanding others through facing ourselves. *Childhood Education* (May): 411–14.

Lerner, H. 1985. *The dance of anger: A woman's guide to changing the patterns of intimate relationships.* New York: Harper and Row.

Paley, V. G. 2000. *White teacher.* Cambridge, Mass.: Harvard University Press.

Palmer, P. J. 1998. *The courage to teach: Exploring the inner landscape of a teacher's life.* San Francisco: Jossey-Bass.

CHAPTER FOUR

WE FACE OUR FEELINGS OF POWERLESSNESS

A Childcare or Child Welfare Worker's Lament

Lord, I've got too many children and too few hands
too many demands, too long hours and too little rest
too much noise and too little notice
too much tension and too few thanks
never any peace and not enough pay.

I make less than janitors, parking attendants, and garbage
    collectors

though I help mold the human future every day.
Lord, when is our nation going to come to its senses
    and value those who care for our children?

  —MARIAN WRIGHT EDELMAN

Quite recently I was hospitalized for four days to combat an infection. The nurses who took care of me were very efficient in how often they administered the bags of intravenous antibiotics. They were very busy. The ward had a number of rooms, and many of the patients had more urgent medical needs than mine. I was considered ambulatory and well enough to take care of myself in a number of ways. I appreciated the nurses' efficiency and competence as they rushed in and out of my room to tend to my medical situation. But I felt emotionally invisible. In the first place, as I had not been admitted to a hospital for more than twenty years, it was a stressful situation for me. In addition to simply not feeling well because of fever and some pain, I was anxious about my medical condition, not knowing where it would lead or how long it would take to get better.

After two days of efficient medical attention, I realized suddenly that I was feeling lonely, isolated, and invisible. It really was not anyone's fault, for the nurses were doing what they needed to do to take care of me medically and physically. They just never seemed to address me by name, nor did they take the time to ask how I was or who I was or find out anything about me in a more personal way. Indeed, I was missing personal and emotional interactions. On the third day, I started delaying the nurses after their short, brusque visits to hook up the antibiotics, read my blood pressure, or take my temperature. I asked them how they were feeling, expressed interest in their personal lives, and encouraged them to share stories about themselves. I discovered that one of the nurses was also studying law, was married, and had a young child. Another had just been to New York City over the weekend and was excited to share stories about visiting with her grandchild. By the time I left the hospital the nurses were slowly starting to ask me about myself too. I learned they were interesting, diverse, complex women with busy and somewhat stressful lives. They did not mean to ignore my emotional needs. Their lives and work got in the way.

The nurses reminded me of the teachers and caregivers in the campus child care center where I was a director for eleven years. These were strong, competent, and dedicated women who worked tirelessly with our youngest children, ages six weeks to five years. Often having to put aside complex and stressful personal lives, they would throw themselves into caring for and educating the tender, vulnerable children in their classrooms. At times they showed that same amazing efficiency with their physical chores that I experienced in the hospital with the nurses. Nevertheless, when the teachers became busy making order out of the chaos that sometimes accompanies an early childhood classroom, as their supervisor I often had to remind them not to forget or ignore the children's emotional needs.

CHILD CARE WORKERS SUFFER FROM SOCIETY'S PERCEPTIONS OF THEM AND HAVE TO DEAL WITH THE RESULTING EMOTIONS.

Harsh versus Compassionate Caregiving

As I was preparing for this writing project, a colleague sent me a book as a gift. She talked with me at length about her concern for what she described as "harsh caregiving," which she witnessed occurring in a number of early childhood programs. With great courage to confront her own behaviors and emotions, she had realized with dismay that she herself had often been a harsh caregiver while working with toddlers in a child care setting many years prior. My colleague had coined the phrase "harsh caregiving" as opposed to "emotionally, responsive, empowering caregiving," which is used in the book she had given me (Leavitt 1994). She is now determined to study, write about, and support teachers in becoming emotionally responsive caregivers.

Each time I start reading excerpts from Leavitt's book, I become choked up with tears of rage, empathy, and dismay from the various descriptions of field notes about the children's experiences in child care settings. For example:

> " The caregiver was hovering over Andrea's crib, vigorously shaking it. . . . Andrea (seven months) was curled up into a ball in the corner of her crib, crying. The caregiver continued to shake her crib for about ten minutes. She then picked up Andrea and put her on the tile floor in front of the crib. She said, 'If you won't go to sleep, then you can just sit there,' and then walked away. . . . A while later, Andrea was rubbing her eyes as she lay on the floor. The caregiver picked her up and changed her diaper. She took Andrea and laid her in her crib. Andrea instantly began to cry. The caregiver began to shake the crib. This continued for a while. The caregiver did not talk soothingly to Andrea or pat her back. Another caregiver came over and observed the situation. She picked Andrea up and sat with her in the rocking chair. In about ten minutes Andrea fell asleep. This caregiver placed her gently in her crib where she continued to sleep. " (Leavitt 1994, 63)

At times my pain at reading some of the descriptions of caregiving situations becomes so acute, I find that I must put the book down and make myself a cup of tea before I am able to proceed. Sometimes I weep. I am not sure if I feel pain for those times when I was a child curled up in a ball somewhere crying alone, bewildered, or afraid, or if it is because I have witnessed similar scenes like these in different child care settings where I have been a consultant, validator, or visitor. Indeed, I have from time to time witnessed harsh caregiving in my own child care center when I was the director. Mostly I weep because I know that those field notes and descriptions of the children's experiences are true and ongoing. Leavitt describes child care as "emotional labor" that becomes burdensome especially because caregivers are expected to "emotionally engage intensely" and that to be "other-directed for such long hours can create considerable emotional strain on [their] capacities to care for the children" (Leavitt 1994, 61). Leavitt further describes that "in one of the few studies examining working conditions in day care centers . . . one-fourth of the caregivers mentioned dealing with children as something they liked least about their job" (Leavitt 1994, 62).

Society's View of Our Profession

Children's challenging behaviors are not the only cause of teachers' anger and frustration. Sometimes our place in the hierarchy of our profession makes us angry and resentful. Early childhood teachers in child care settings work long, hard hours and are the lowest paid people in the education profession. Not only that—most of society views caregivers as "just a bunch of women watching a bunch of kids" (Jacobson 2003, 72). Some states, more recently, are realizing the importance of education in the early years. They are showing their awareness by funding and reinforcing prekindergarten programs for four-year-olds. However, they still do not believe infant, toddler, and three-year-old care and education are important enough to require that caregivers have quality education or a decent living wage. These types of conditions lower our sense of self-worth and cause resentment.

When I think back to when I was director of the campus child care center, I realize that teachers and caregivers often feel powerless and underappreciated. First, there is the lack of respect from society for the work that they do. Second, they are often excluded from the decision-making process of the administration on issues such as numbers of children enrolled in their classrooms or when children move to different age groups. Then there is the "drudgery of routine tasks such as diaper changing and feeding which are repeated endlessly" (Leavitt 1994, 63), the hard work of constantly lifting children, the frequency of contracting illnesses, and the stress of children crying.

> " As caregivers face the constant, unpredictable, and demanding needs of the children, they may feel a sense of diminishing control and the loss of their own individual autonomy. They may be driven to exert control where they can—on powerless children. The caregiver's inflexibility, then, may stem partly from their own needs for control and predictability. " (Leavitt 1994, 47)

I often wonder how women in the child care profession came to choose the work they do. For example, I was one of those people who chose early childhood partly because I did not believe I could do anything else. It was almost as if there were no other options available to me. If child care does not require appropriate levels of education, and the pay is less than what garbage collectors earn, then it must follow that anyone can do it! Starting with this type of low view of myself and the profession, it was often hard to lift myself out of feelings of low self-worth and powerlessness. I have discovered I am not alone in these experiences. Even those who consciously choose the profession because they believe they can make a difference in children's lives must work hard at not allowing the societal view or hard, emotional labor that Leavitt describes to bring their self-esteem down. Recently, one of my undergraduate early childhood students reflected on this issue in a paper she prepared for a course I taught. She wrote:

> " I never realized how under-appreciated many women feel in the early childhood field as a result of societal pressures in a patriarchal society which further affects their relationships with students and their parents. Growing up I was fortunate enough at least to have an extremely caring and supportive family. For as long as I can remember my parents have always encouraged me to pursue my dream and provide me with the support I need to obtain my personal and educational goals. In the past I have recognized that men do have many more advantages than women in society, however, I have never let that stop me from reaching for what I want. I strive to be the best at whatever I do, and I refuse to let anyone put me down because I want to be able to help children to develop a good sense of self-worth like I have, so they too, can feel invincible in a demanding and challenging society. "

All of this is well and good if, in fact, early childhood teachers and caregivers actually consciously chose the profession. Even this student, who has chosen the profession for the most noble of reasons, will most likely have to work tirelessly at not allowing the societal point of view or the relentless emotional labor of caring for young children to pull down her level of confidence. Too often, the result is burnout, which leads caregivers to leave the preschool ages to become a "real" teacher of older children.

Women and Strong Emotions

" Women, however, have long been discouraged from the awareness and forthright expression of anger. Sugar and spice are the ingredients from which we are made. We are the nurturers, the soothers, the peacemakers, and the steadiers of rocked boats. We may hold relationships in place as if our lives depended on it. . . . Anger is a tool for change when it challenges us to become more of an expert on the self and less of an expert on others. " (Lerner 1985)

As I write this book, for the first time the country is seriously contemplating a woman for president. During the campaigning for the recent primaries, I received an e-mail from a friend who explained she intended to support and vote for a female president with all her might. She explained she would not be able to live with herself if she did not, because, as a feminist, she was concerned it could be many years before this opportunity came around again.

Recently I read an opinion piece about voting for a female president (Steinem 2008) as well as an article describing how men and women are viewed in the workplace (Belkin 2007). Both articles made me think about how difficult it had been for me to believe I had the ability and the right not only to acquire a higher education but also to be forceful and assertive when I needed to be. I was clearly socialized to believe that men owned the intellectual sphere and workplace. In my first book, *Confronting Our Discomfort,* I describe how a faculty member of my alma mater termed me a "bitch" because I stood up for myself about how I was being treated by my advisor (Jacobson 2003). There have been many times during my professional career that I have had a hard time being taken seriously or, indeed, knowing how to balance being assertive with being compassionate and nurturing. Still, I must say, we have come quite a long way—a little more than eighty years ago, women in the United States were not even allowed to vote. Even so, I was dismayed at how much the media talked about Hillary Rodham Clinton when, at a point in her primary election campaign, she became tearful while speaking passionately about why she was running for president.

From an early age young girls are socialized to repress expressions, or even feelings, of anger. Subsequently, if women in the workplace become assertive or strong and express their feelings, they are called derogatory names. In Belkin's article and in Steinem's opinion piece, these stereotypes and expectations relate specifically to women in positions of leadership competing with men for positions of power. In a nurturing profession like child care and education, where there are few to almost no men to compete with, women are expected to be even more nurturing, sweet, and kind. After all, aren't all "women who watch a bunch of kids" naturally kind and caring? At the same time, we are expected to discipline children and teach them how to behave according to the norms of society. What a dilemma! How are we expected to set clear and firm boundaries for children and at the same time remain kind and nurturing? The confusion is understandable, for being assertive and strong are not qualities that are seen as positive attributes for women. Mostly we praise little girls for being pretty or caring. Very seldom do we tell them that we admire their strength or intelligence. Discipline and setting boundaries are all about being assertive. I have long grappled with the notion that assertiveness and strength are considered unkind. Meanness and disrespect are unkind. Yet setting clear limits nurtures safety for children.

Caregivers work hard at a profession that is undervalued, and they are expected to be nurturing and emotionally responsive while feeling resentment, low self-worth, and powerlessness. It should come as no surprise that when caregivers find themselves in situations where they feel helpless and frustrated, they are more likely to release anger in inappropriate ways with children, who have even less power. There are all manner of reasons for caregivers, most of whom are women, to feel angry or resentful. Some teachers have told me that they have repressed emotions for so long that they cannot tell when or if they are angry. They have to work hard at self-reflection to realize that they are feeling anything at all because they have learned to deny certain emotions since they were children.

ACTIONS TO TAKE

Consider These Questions

- How did you choose to become a teacher of young children?
- What or who influenced your choosing a caregiving profession?
- How has repressing your emotions, especially those seemingly dangerous and unacceptable ones like anger

and resentment, affected you in allowing children to express theirs?

- How do we empower children when we feel powerless
  ourselves?
- How do you know when you are being a harsh and not
  emotionally responsive caregiver?
- How do you feel about women being assertive and
  strong?
- How do your feelings of confidence and lack of confidence affect your daily interactions with children and
  families?

Simply considering these questions might not be enough, because some of the answers you uncover for yourself will make you
angry or could even cause you pain. It helps to talk them out with
someone. My friend who wrote me the e-mail about being a feminist supporting Hillary Rodham Clinton deals with these types of
questions and feelings by being an advocate for women's rights.
Channeling the pain and anger into a fight for social justice is a
productive way of taking action. Whenever I become passionate
about these types of issues, my husband reminds me of a saying:
"Don't mourn. Organize!" Writing in my blog helped me work out
my feelings when I wrote about the recent election campaign:

> "I am aghast at all the sexist rhetoric about Hillary Clinton.
> Not because I did not know it exists. Sexism is alive and
> very well all over the world, including the United States of
> America. When Hillary is passionate, strong, confident, and
> assertive, she is termed aggressive, too angry, and I can only
> imagine what else! Not so for the male candidates. After I
> heard about an incident with Hillary today I passionately

and assertively charged into my study to write this down. Signs were held up while she was speaking stating: 'Stick to ironing.' I rather prefer a bumper sticker I have seen lately that states: 'A woman's place is in the White House!'

I would vote for Hillary in a heart beat. She is intelligent, professional, and has so much political experience. While I watch the struggle and challenges she faces as a woman running this race, my heart reaches out to her and feelings surge for all women to gather together and rise up as one to push her through—our life sister. I ached to see her short show of emotion yesterday dragged across the media over and over again. As if showing emotion is something to be guarded against in this Patriarchal system, where men and women alike wallow and self-destruct. 'You see?' I can hear people say. 'That's what happens if you vote for a woman. She will just let her emotions get in the way!'

As if it doesn't ever happen to all those seemingly rational, dominant men out there! "

Writing publicly in that manner helped me review my feelings. In addition, different people commented about what I had written, turning it all into a productive debate at the time.

In the past, sometimes writing a letter without actually sending it has helped me to articulate difficult feelings. Many years ago I wrote just such a letter that I did not send. It was addressed to my mother and father, who had divorced, telling them what it felt like being their daughter (Jacobson 2003, 124–25). I had learned this technique from one of my therapists, who suggested I write a letter to my father after he had died. At that time, I was full of regret that I had not been able to tell him how much I loved him. Over the years I have written in my journal other letters that I have not sent or shared publicly. Writing such personal letters helped me to process anger, grief, or feelings of injustice.

As you consider the questions listed on pages 82–83, you might address a letter to society, the administration of your school district, your center director, the principal, or even the president of the country! You could start the letter by saying, "Dear (whomever you choose)." Remember to write out everything you feel. Let all the frustration and rage out onto the paper. I have known people to burn those letters afterward, bury them in the ground, or keep them locked up in a private box until they no longer felt they needed them. Lately, I think I might like to write such a letter to "Patriarchy." I would start it: "Dear Patriarchy, where dominance reigns supreme, everyone is rational, and emotional expression is considered a weakness." Who knows? The letter could eventually be sent to a legislator or published in a public newsletter.

Making a stand for ourselves is important in our work with young children. When we feel strong and confident, we are less likely to feel threatened, resentful, or angry. We have more space to be open and emotionally available for children. In addition, we are more able to accept their diverse opinions and assertive behaviors. When we feel strong, confident, and in control of our life choices, we are more likely to empower others while having less need to control them.

CONCLUSION

Power structures in our profession affect how we feel. As an early childhood teacher educator I can tell you that it becomes difficult to convince young, ambitious women to remain in the child care profession for extended periods of time. No doubt about it, you have to be committed and dedicated to do this work. Pay is low, and the societal view is biased. The perception that it is "just a bunch of women watching a bunch of kids" is pervasive. It seeps into our consciousness and lowers our confidence level. So many undergraduate students tell me that they want to become "real" teachers—referring to anything higher than preschool. We are slowly whittling down these perceptions by informing legislators and administrators about the importance of care and education in the early years. But we still have a long way to go.

Recently I was talking on the phone with a dear friend. She told me that her sister, who is a prominent children's author, sends the books that she writes about learning to read to local legislators and even the president of the country where she resides. When we discussed the recent election campaigns and I told her who I was voting for, my friend said excitedly, "Send your books to them, Tam!" I gasped, "I couldn't do that!" "Why not?" she asked, laughing out loud. "Who am *I* to send *my* books to such prominent and important people?" I replied sheepishly.

"There I go, in and out of confidence again," I thought to myself when the telephone conversation had ended. Legislators and even the president are just people too! We are all in this life together—men, women, and children—and who knows? Perhaps some of what I have to say might influence a person more powerful than I am, have an impact, and affect change for children and teachers in the future. Working with young children and their families has always seemed like a noble and important profession to me, no matter what I was paid, no matter what our patriarchal society thought of me. And yet, time after time, feeling unappreciated or unacknowledged weighed me down and shook my confidence level.

For some reason, as I write this, I am reminded of one of my favorite pieces by Robert Fulghum, one describing "an old woman, an Albanian who grew up in Yugoslavia; she is a Roman Catholic nun who lives in poverty in India," as he looks at a photograph of Mother Teresa receiving the Nobel Peace Prize in Oslo in 1980 (Fulghum 1988, 189). Some years later he sees her again as a guest at a conference of quantum physicists and religious mystics in Bombay and describes her as "one simple woman in a faded sari and worn sandals" (Fulghum 1988, 191). He writes:

> She strode to the rostrum and changed the agenda of the conference from intellectual inquiry to moral activism. She said in a firm voice to the awed assembly: 'We can do no great things; only small things with great love. . . .'
>
> And while I wrestle with frustration about the impotence of the individual, she goes right on changing the world. While I *wish* for more power and resources, she *uses* her power and resources to do what she can do at the moment. (Fulghum 1988, 192)

Fulghum's words have always inspired me. As women or caregivers, we really do not have much time to wallow in self-pity or feel like victims of society. In our work, young children need us to be present, emotionally available, strong, and confident for them. We need all our personal power and whatever resources at our disposal to do what we can do at the moment. And then, maybe, we can, with great love, turn those small children in our care into great human beings!

References

Belkin, L. 2007. The feminine critique. *New York Times*, November 1, http://www.nytimes.com/.

Edelman, M. W. 1995. *Guide my feet: Prayers and meditations on loving and working for children*. Boston: Beacon.

Fulghum, R. 1988. *All I really need to know I learned in kindergarten: Uncommon thoughts on common things*. New York: Villard Books.

Jacobson, T. 2003. *Confronting our discomfort: Clearing the way for anti-bias in early childhood*. Portsmouth, N.H.: Heinemann.

Leavitt, R. L. 1994. *Power and emotion in infant-toddler day care*. Albany: State University of New York Press.

Lerner, H. G. 1985. *The dance of anger: A woman's guide to changing the patterns of intimate relationships*. New York: Harper and Row.

Steinem, G. 2008. Women are never front-runners. *New York Times*, January 8, http://www.nytimes.com/.

CHAPTER FIVE

WE CLAIM OUR OWN
CHILDHOOD TRAUMAS

*We do not actually learn from experience as much as we
learn from reflecting on experience.*

—GEORGE J. POSNER

*[Reflection is] the practice of intentionally bringing into
conscious awareness one's motivations, thoughts, beliefs,
questions, assumptions, feelings, attitudes, desires, and
expectations for the purpose of gaining insightful understanding as to their meaning, their connections to what is
personally known, and in light of new experiences and information. Reflection makes possible the insights necessary
to learn from experience and alter habitual behaviors.*

—MARIANNE JONES AND MARILYN SHELTON

Adults create emotionally stressful experiences for children perhaps because they do not remember their own childhood past. By remembering their own needs and vulnerabilities during childhood, caregivers may learn to recognize and respond to those of children (Bowman 1989). Exploring the meanings of responsive caregiving for caregivers then becomes an "intensely personal affair" (Giroux 1981) as caregivers delve into their own childhoods, their own biographies. For caregivers, then, inquiry into the meaning of responsive caregiving is a process of self-inquiry and reflection as well as self-care. Caregivers must become more self-aware, as well as child aware, and comfortable with their own and the children's emotionality. . . . Self-awareness and self-care also require self-acceptance on the part of the caregiver.

—Robin Lynn Leavitt

When my son was six or seven, I was afraid that others would be critical of me because I was a single parent. In fact, I felt ashamed that I was divorced, as if I had failed in some way and was a bad person. I connected that to a number of different incidents growing up. Once, for example, someone at school said that I came from a broken home because my mother had divorced and re-married, and when I came home from school, I asked her about it. I always remember my mother's indignation and alarm when I asked her if I was from a "broken home." I assumed that I had offended her and internalized that it must be a very bad thing to be from a broken home. When my son was young, I had the good fortune to work in a one-room preschool house for the same hours that my son attended his kindergarten class. I would arrive home one hour after he did, however, because he could walk from school directly across the road from our home, and I had to ride my bicycle across town. We lived in a large housing development with long, low tenement buildings, where neighbors were friendly and helpful and the community was safe for children to play in the large playground in the quad directly outside our apartment.

My son had his key to let himself into our home, and he knew the instructions to stay and play in his room until I returned. I did not want him playing outside motherless, for fear of the neighbors thinking I was a neglectful parent or noting that he came from a broken home. One day, I came home to find him playing outdoors with the neighbors' children. Their parents were sitting on benches close by, and he was completely safe. But I saw red! I was enraged and anxious. Needless to say I must have appeared terrifyingly angry to my son. After I shouted at him and spanked him on his bottom, we came into the apartment. He went to his room to play while I prepared lunch. He was subdued, and I was shaken up. I could not understand the intensity of my anger. After all, I knew the neighbors well, and I was sure that he was safe. And then I realized that mostly I was ashamed—afraid that the neighbors would think of me as "that single mom with a latchkey kid from a broken home," neglectful and unfit as a mother. I apologized to my son and explained to him why I had been so angry.

For a long time after that I struggled with the fact that I spanked my son a few times in his childhood. A few years ago I found this passage by Alice Miller. As I read it, I wept:

66 When I read of the recent progress in brain research and the results of the work being done on early infancy, it helped me to realize why the effects of those first lessons and

messages are so persistent. Armed with this new information, I would say to mothers today: 'Don't be distressed
if you find yourselves involuntarily giving your children a
smack. It's something your hand learned very early on; it
happens almost automatically, and you can usually limit the
damage by recognizing that you made a mistake and admit-
ting your error. But whatever you do, don't ever tell your
children you hit them for their own good. If you do, you
will be contributing to the perpetuation of willful stupidity
and covert sadism.' " (Miller 2001, 116)

A few moments after I finished writing about the incident with
my son, the telephone rang. It was my son, now age thirty-four,
calling me from his home in Boston. I laughed as I saw his call-back
number and answered immediately, saying joyously, "Hey, hello
there! I was just writing about you in my book!" He inquired what
I had written about, and I described the situation, asking if he remembered the details of it the way I had. He was silent for a short
moment and then said he did not. He did, however, remember that
one night, around that time period, we were driving home from visiting a friend of mine, and I promised him that I would never spank
him again. Now I fell silent.

"How did you feel when I said that to you? Can you remember
that far back?" I asked.

"Good question," he replied. There was more silence as my
son, a grown man, reflected back on being age six or seven.

"I appreciated it," he said. "I thought that it was very good
that you promised it. I felt that you showed me that you didn't feel
good with what you did." He paused and then continued, "I have
always remembered it—it influenced me and stood out for me. I felt

safer from then on. I always knew somehow even if you were angry that at least that wouldn't happen to me again."

WE CANNOT ESCAPE THE PATTERNS WE EXPERIENCED, BUT WE CAN RESPOND WITH INTELLIGENT AWARENESS RATHER THAN KNEE-JERK REACTIONS.

Young children's emotions are intense. I think of their emotional expressions as primitive and raw. Children are not yet sophisticated or controlled like adults, and therefore tend to blurt out whatever it is they are feeling or thinking without holding back. When that happens, our own childhood memory can awaken or trigger spontaneous reactions that seem to come from nowhere and make us feel out of control. For example, have you ever felt that suddenly you are saying something just like what your mother or father said when you were a child? This has happened to me many times. The words just seem to come out of my mouth without my control. While this is not always a negative occurrence (for my mother said many interesting and wonderful things while I was growing up), it still feels as if I have no control of what comes out of my mouth. Alice Miller describes this phenomenon further:

66 I never cease to be amazed by the precision with which people often reproduce their parents' behavior, although they have no memory of their own early childhoods. A father will beat his son and humiliate him with sarcastic remarks but not have any memory whatsoever of having been

similarly humiliated by his own father. Only in a searching therapeutic context will he (ideally) recall what happened to him at the same age. Merely forgetting early traumas and early neglect is no solution. The past always catches up with us, in our relationships with other people and especially with our children. " (Miller 2001, 124)

Collecting data about my reactions or interactions helps me understand my feelings in a way that gives me a sense of control in a seemingly chaotic situation. I am then able to *choose* how I will behave or interact, and not simply react from unconscious ancient memories, associations, or pain that seems to jump out of nowhere when I least expect it. It is something I do to develop my sense of self. Simply put, it is good for me! One of my favorite authors, Harriet Lerner, describes self-reflection as "self-loving":

" Anxiety, by its very nature, will lead you to lose objectivity about the complex, wonderful, flawed, ever-changing person you are. When you can't see yourself objectively, you won't see anyone else objectively either. . . . Nobody is perfect, and we can all benefit from working on ourselves. But the process of self-observation, reflection, and change is basically a self-loving task. " (Lerner 2004)

Children's Lack of Control over Circumstances

I have always been curious about what makes me tick. It is fascinating. Trying to figure it out is almost like a detective story. I love to prod and pry into the whys and wherefores of how I came to be me and how or why other people function the way they do. Looking back, I think I developed this type of curiosity in order to feel as though I had some kind of control over my life. It was an illusion of course. There was much that was out of my control. For example, when I was a child, I had no control over my parents' divorce, their remarriages, or my having to live with a stepfather instead of my biological father. Nor did I have control over my placement in the family, fourth out of five children, half-sibling to everyone because my siblings had different fathers. Children have no control over these types of life events. They are pushed and pulled through situations, and they develop unique ways to survive them. I was a child like that. I developed a keen sense of observation so that I would know how people perceived me and what I needed to do in order to please others, so that I might fit in and be acceptable to them. In short, I did everything I could to make people love me.

Not feeling as though I belonged anywhere, I became an observing outsider—listening, noticing, and interpreting. In fact, it was the very act of interpreting that gave me the illusion of control—a feeling of power when, in fact, I was powerless. It was as if I knew what people were thinking and feeling about me and thus could feel safe knowing how to behave in ways that I thought others would want. This heightened sensitivity to others became a significant skill in my work later in life, and I have been able to put it to good use. But there was also another, more painful side to it. I felt I was to blame for the way other people were feeling, especially because I was told time and again that I was "destroying" my mother and being a nuisance to my stepfather when I expressed myself emotionally. I caused people to feel whatever it was they were feeling—that all had to be because of all-powerful little me! So while I had developed illusions of control to compensate for feelings of helplessness, I had also turned those very same feelings against myself, making myself feel bad because I was *seemingly* responsible for others' emotions.

Years later, in therapy, I realized with relief that I did not have such a magical, awesome power, whether for good or for bad. The truth is that the significant adults in my life when I was a child were responsible for their own feelings. My mother would say things to me like, "You are destroying me" or "You are annoying your stepfather" in order to stop me from expressing myself emotionally and not because there was any truth or reality to what I was actually doing. A young child having a tantrum cannot, in fact, destroy anyone. As a young child, I believed that I was the cause of my parents' anger, anxiety, or grief. As I grew older, I transferred those feelings to my personal relations or to people I worked with. Just as young children learn how to survive physically, they develop emotional survival skills very early in their lives.

" Most of what we learned was acquired unconsciously, through trial and error, by observing significant adults in our lives navigating fears of discomfort and stress. We learned to survive in our family systems and communities. Our survival depended on doing the right things so that people we cared about would like us. Adults around us taught us what was safe or dangerous through their praise, admonishments, and silence. Nonverbal communication is subtle. It could be a tightening of the lips, an angry or anxious glance, slight shifting of the body, or a foot quivering back and forth. Children quickly learn to differentiate between the nonverbal cues that are safe or not reliable. They make assumptions based on what they sense unless we are explicit in what we mean. " (Jacobson 2003, 44)

How We Were Disciplined as Young Children

When I facilitate workshops on behavior management for early childhood professionals, people share ways that they were disciplined when they were growing up. Some of the punishments include: being told they were bad or to "shut up" because children were not allowed to participate in adult conversations occurring while they were present; getting "the look"; receiving spankings and beatings with hands, switches, belts, or wooden spoons; experiencing belittling words like, "How can you be so stupid?" or being told that girls are not smart enough; having their mouths washed out with soap; being forced to kneel on rice for periods of time; being sent to their room; not receiving dessert or dinner; being pinched, pushed, or dragged by the arms; having their hair pulled; and being slapped in the face, especially for "answering back." Some describe how they had to go into the backyard and choose the switch for their imminent beating. For almost two decades, undergraduate students in my child development classes each semester have described similar experiences when asked about discipline in their childhood. It does not matter whether they are professionals in workshops or students in college classes, whether they are young or old or rich or poor, or what their cultural background happens to be. The list remains constant over the years. I write up word for word every expression of discipline that people remember and then ask them to look at the list and tell us what it makes them think about.

As they look at the list of punishments written up on the blackboard, invariably a silence comes over the room. When I ask them what they see about what they have said, without exception they reply, "Abuse." Some say it out loud, indignantly. Others mouth the word silently or let it slip out like a whisper, as if they do not want anyone to hear them. At times, the word "abuse" is accompanied by nervous laughter. As early childhood caregivers and educators, they have a sense of shame attached to saying it out loud, even though these are things that happened to them when they were children—things that they had no control over, for which they were and are not to blame.

I think about a young woman who recently attended one of my workshops. She told how, when she was a child, her mother had come to her school and dragged her through the halls, pulling her while dragging her hair along the ground, because she had been told her daughter had behaved badly. This same young woman was finding it very difficult to treat her own small daughter in a compassionate way. Indeed, she could not even imagine how being kind could work in disciplining her child. She became most indignant when I suggested that I like to warn children ahead of time before I wipe their nose. As I was describing kneeling at the child's eye level and saying, "I am going to wipe your nose now," instead of just coming up and cleaning his nose without warning, the woman in the audience became agitated. She called out, interrupting me, "Oh yeah, right! Like I am going to warn my four-year-old before I wipe her nose! I don't think so!" And then she proceeded to tell us the story of how her own mother had pulled her down the hallway at school with her hair dragging on the ground.

A student recently described how, when she was a young child, her mother would secretly pinch her if she was acting disruptively in public places. One time she was in the mall with her mother and a friend. The mother mistook the friend to be her daughter and pinched her by mistake. She immediately apologized. The student who shared this story, a woman in her twenties, expressed not a small amount of indignation that her mother had never once apologized to her as she did to her friend for pinching her in that manner. She vowed that she would never treat her future children like that.

How do we imagine that early childhood disciplinary experiences such as these have not affected adults teaching young children? Some might choose to repeat what was done to them because they believe it worked. They feel frustrated because discipline policies dictate different strategies, like the woman in my workshop who was dragged across the school hallway. Some might decide to do it differently and make changes in the ways they set boundaries for children in the future, like the student in my class who was pinched in secret and never received an apology. Our earliest emotional memories remain with us throughout our lives and affect how we feel in situations that remind us of how we were treated.

As we start to reflect on discipline and our own early childhoods, it is important to identify the connections we make between our own experiences of pain or fear with those behaviors that cause us the most discomfort. Recently a colleague and fellow expert in early childhood education was overheard talking about how she does not appreciate children's fantasy play. As she thought about it further, she mused out loud that perhaps it had to do with being influenced by growing up during the Second World War, when her life was serious, dangerous, and stressful. For her, fantasy play in those frightening times must have seemed frivolous, inappropriate. For others, fantasy play might have been comforting to enable an escape from the disturbing reality around them.

Some children seem to be more sensitive than others, or perhaps more resilient. I know that when I was a child, I was deeply influenced by one or two incidents of harsh treatment when I misbehaved. For example, to this day, fifty-five years later, I can still conjure up the taste of the soap that was used to wash my mouth out when I was four or five years old. My older siblings had taught me some juicy curse words, and I was not afraid to try them out one day when we were out in public at the circus. Having my mouth washed out with soap was quite terrifying, I must say, and I did not curse again until I was an adult. Even now, I feel uncomfortable and not a little evil when I use such words.

Discipline is only one aspect of what has influenced our adult behaviors, but it is an important piece of the puzzle that makes up our whole selves. If we disobeyed our parents, we risked not only punishment but also the fear of abandonment, which is terrifying for young children. The people we needed so desperately for their love, acknowledgment, or approval when we were young taught us what was dangerous and important for our emotional survival. Much of what they shared with us was essential for learning socialization skills so that we could function successfully within the community. On the other hand, some of their teachings were fraught with their own fears and anxieties and were not relevant to who we were or to the period or social class into which we were born. For example, a child growing up in an environment of deprivation has emotional survival experiences different from those of a child in an environment of plenty. In the same way, people who struggled to survive emotionally and financially in the past will have different kinds of anxieties and concerns bringing up their children in the present than those whose lives seemed safe and peaceful.

Validating Our Feelings

" Only by knowing the truth can we be set free. Only in this way can we free ourselves from the fears and anxieties we knew as children, blamed and punished for sins we did not know we had committed, the fateful fear of the sin of disobedience, that crippling anxiety that has wrecked so many people's lives and keeps them in thrall to their own childhood. *"* (Miller 2001, 9)

Finding out about our emotional history takes time. Some of it we do by tapping into our feelings as they are happening then and there with children acting out in our classrooms. Writing it down and reflecting on these incidents later can help us understand why this or that emotion was triggered, the relevance of the degree of intensity of feeling, or the efficacy of our interactions and strategies. We map out our own emotional development stories. Asking ourselves questions is one way of making connections or deepening an understanding about our history. For example, where did we learn, what do we understand about, or how did we interpret kindness, courage, and compassion?

For me it was always intriguing—a kind of mystery—how I learned kindness. I recall learning about it from observing the actions of family members or strangers either with others or directly with me. What people said to me did not hold as much weight as their actions, and I certainly did not trust people who said one thing but did the opposite. It was always important to me that people "walked their talk." As I grow older, I realize that life is more complicated than what I had always thought. People often deeply believe what they say even though they are unable to carry it through for all sorts of reasons, including fear of intimacy, anxiety in general, being unaware or in denial, or simply being stuck in a developmental stage that holds them back. I no longer interpret their inability to act as being in opposition to what they say they feel.

As adults explore the history of their emotional development, it is important for them to validate their own feelings. When we acknowledge that these events took place and that they were hurtful for us, we are able to take them out into the open and examine them closely. We might go through a few stages in the realization process, including anger at that ancient pain or sadness at the loss of illusion about how we thought about our parents when we were children. These stages become necessary for allowing us to forgive our parents later and deepen our love and appreciation of them as the complex human beings they are.

To deny ourselves this process is to pretend that what happened to us was not true or that we made it all up just to be difficult—to make trouble. As a result, we will undoubtedly believe that the young children in our classrooms are making up their feelings too. How will we believe them if we do not believe ourselves? Many of us are wounded children and were put in the impossible situation of being hurt or humiliated by the very people we loved and depended upon for survival. When we were children, we felt fear, confusion, shame, exclusion, guilt, anger, sadness, disappointment, jealousy, frustration, exuberance, or joy about all sorts of situations, events, and interactions. To make matters more complicated, significant adults in our lives repeatedly told us how we *should* feel about what was happening. And so we learned to doubt our own feelings or, in the worst cases, to doubt that painful events we remember even happened at all. We have a right to acknowledge those old painful experiences from childhood, however small they might seem to us now that we are adults. As teachers of young children, we have a responsibility to understand our feelings. Only then will we be able to validate children's feelings too.

"Learn to believe that your memories matter," says John Bradshaw (1990). When we learn to validate our feelings and experiences, our parents' intentions are not relevant to our story. Our parents might have stopped us from weeping because they wanted us to be strong. And, because they were taught to repress their grief, many adults still need to learn to fully express themselves through their tears.

> " Believe me: a lot of what you were told was legitimate parenting was actually abuse. If you're still inclined to minimize and/or rationalize the ways in which you were shamed, ignored, or used to nurture your parents, you need now to accept the fact that these things truly wounded your soul. " (Bradshaw 1990, 77)

Sometimes when people do this kind of self-reflection, they might feel shocked or fearful about being disloyal to their families. These feelings crop up even if they are only thinking to themselves, and some level of dismay is especially likely when people share their stories with others. Time and again when students or teachers at in-service trainings share publicly their memories about painful punishments or humiliation in their childhood, they ask me jokingly not to tell their parents what they have said. They call out from the audience or classrooms, "I hope you are not going to tell our parents that we said all these things!" I take the joke seriously and reply that I will not tell their parents what they have said. In fact, I take seriously most things that adults share with me about their earliest memories, even if they are laughing as they speak about what they report. Any degree of humiliation or childhood pain is serious. It has inevitably left behind smaller or larger scars that have an impact on a person's perceptions and ways of interacting with others.

Taking these things seriously is one way of validating a person's feelings. But I do not believe we can ever really know what it is like to walk in someone else's shoes. Our life experiences, personalities, memories, cultural histories, or sensitivities are simply too different from one another. Each of us is unique. We might have an idea or inkling of another's experiences, but we can never *really* know what it is like to be that person in that particular situation at that particular time. Nevertheless, we can at least take people seriously when they tell us such personal stories. We can believe them even when what they describe sounds impossible. We can remember that such events are real, even though they may not be in our realm of experience—that is to say, they never could have happened to us.

A Never-Ending Process

Validating our feelings or taking our emotional memories seriously means that we listen to ourselves. As we collect data about our feelings, actions, and memories, we analyze them as critically as we would anyone else's. We observe ourselves, start to take notice of what we feel when, and ask questions of ourselves and others. This is not a one-time event. It is ongoing and probably lasts forever. It always accompanies us as we work with children and their families.

About a week after I had begun writing this chapter, I was out in my yard raking leaves. It was a brisk, cold day, and my work became quite strenuous as I threw myself into the task, eagerly negotiating the wind whirling the leaves up and around me as I raked. As I worked, I was thinking about what I had been writing. My thoughts drifted back and forth and around and about, seemingly uncontrollably—just like those swirling leaves. I think this is often how thoughts work, going from one to another, associatively latching onto memories that make us think of something else and then something different again. As I raked, it felt as if my thoughts had no direct or organized sequence. And yet, somehow, when I reviewed them later, I was able to understand how I went from noticing the swirling leaves to an understanding about my childhood relationship with my mother. In fact, it felt a bit like a revelation, like a thought I had not had so clearly before. Certainly, I have thought about our relationship many times in the past! But this time seemed different. I was reminded of a few lines from a poem by T. S. Eliot (1943):

> *We shall not cease from exploration*
> *And the end of all our exploring*
> *Will be to arrive where we started*
> *And know the place for the first time.*

Suddenly, in the middle of pushing the leaves into a large pile, I was overcome with grief. Almost doubling over in pain, I stopped what I was doing, leaned on the rake, and wept for a few minutes. It occurred to me then and there that when I was a very young child, I loved my mother very much. I adored her. I loved how she looked and smelled. I most especially loved her hands. They were strong and firm and in my eyes, the most beautiful hands I had ever seen. In fact, when I was eight and my mother was in the hospital giving birth to my younger brother, I insisted on staying with a certain friend of hers. I chose this woman because her hands resembled my mother's so much. As I cried out there, holding onto the rake, I realized that I had been missing my mother for a very long time.

Our relationship has been difficult, characterized by many challenging moments between us, but loving my mother was never my problem. I realized that I had always *felt* that I was not her priority.

More than that, I felt as if she wanted to be anywhere else, or with anyone else, rather than with me. The only way I can describe the feeling is to liken it to her being a lover who was always dreaming of being with someone else while he was with me! As I felt that old childhood pain rise up in me as if out of nowhere, I realized instantly that in my personal life I had always seemed to choose life partners who made me feel the way I felt with my mother: unlovable and unwanted. Hence, I have had a number of failed marriages. It was almost as if I had needed to repeat, over and over again, that feeling of wanting someone more than they wanted me or loving someone more than they loved me. What a revelation!

Looking back, in reality, my mother did not mean *not* to focus on me. I was the fourth of five siblings and was born not long before her third marriage. When I came along, her life was full of complexity and anxiety. She remarried when I was four, and most of her energy and attention had to go into her new marriage and youngest son at the time. In addition, my mother was still caring for my three older siblings and negotiating relationships with her two former husbands: my father and the father of my older siblings. Unintentionally, I fell through the cracks. There just was not enough emotional availability or time for me. Today, as an adult, this understanding helps me forgive my mother. She did not mean for me to feel that way. She did the very best she could with what she had under difficult conditions. I realize now that she loved me. Life and her being possibly overwhelmed just got in the way!

Not only did my early childhood relationship with my mother affect my personal life choices, it also influenced my relationship with other people's children. I understand why I have always cared so deeply for children who felt marginalized or unloved. More than that, I have always been very good at managing those children whom many teachers consider to be problematic. Somehow I am able to identify with their pain, longing, or feelings of exclusion. I seem to speak their emotional language. This sudden understanding that came upon me as I raked leaves in my yard surprised me. At age fifty-eight, I thought I had worked out and resolved most of my relationship challenges with my mother. I have been researching myself since my early twenties, personally and professionally. At that moment I realized there was still more to uncover. Researching the self takes time—maybe forever!

At times we will make swift progress with revelations and realizations as we uncover new pieces of our selves. At other times we are liable to regress and revert back to old patterned behaviors and feelings that feel comfortable and familiar because they are what we have known all our lives. Back and forth we go, uncovering, understanding, and regressing again—especially if we come upon painful or shameful memories that are too difficult to overcome all at once, then and there. And yet the more we uncover and confront ourselves, the harder it becomes to deny or ignore what we have learned. Self-alteration happens in spite of one's self! More importantly, our decisions become more conscious, intentional, and clear as we guide behavior or choose how to interact with the children in our care.

ACTIONS TO TAKE

Internal Ethnography

Researching the self is a deeply personal process. No one can tell you how to uncover your early childhood memories or which connections to make. There is no right way to do this, nor is there a correct length of time it will take. Every person is unique not only in genetic makeup and life experiences but in the ways he or she has chosen to develop survival skills or defense mechanisms.

We can start becoming aware of the inner emotional life we have developed since we were young children by *observing* our interactions and *noticing* the kinds of behaviors or emotional situations with children that make us most uncomfortable. Making a detailed and deliberate account of our inner feelings is what I would like to call "researching the self." In other words, I am suggesting we become observers of ourselves! Or put another way, we become researchers of our own emotional lives. When we observe and notice, in a deliberate way, our own interactions or what makes us uncomfortable, we are collecting data about ourselves—just as researchers do. Later, we might find some recurring themes or connections between what happened to us when we were children and situations with other people's children in our classrooms. It reminds me of a type of research called "ethnography." This work is similar to research in the field of ethnography, in which the observer also participates in the culture being observed. So, in a sense, I am inviting you to undertake an "internal ethnography" of yourself, in which you participate because it is your own emotional culture and history that you are collecting data about.

Take a look at some of the ways I have used to help me become aware of the emotional makeup of my psyche:

Write about it. As part of my own internal ethnography, I find it helpful to write down what I am feeling about emotionally intense or stressful situations with children. For example, if a young child shouts out, "I hate you!" some adults might feel hurt, insulted, indignant, angry, or frightened. Those words and the manner in which the child is saying them might bring up for the teacher memories of having her mouth washed out with soap for "answering back" to a parent. On the other hand, those words might relate directly with a childhood memory. A teacher might find that she feels hurt and insulted almost as if she herself had reverted to being three or four years old at that moment. As an observer or researcher of self, you could whip out a notepad and jot down quickly some of the feelings or memories to be reflected upon later in more depth.

Interview others. In ethnography the researcher conducts in-depth interviews with the participants in the study. As I explore my own emotional development I often ask myself questions about my own behaviors. Sometimes I even ask them out loud! I remember feeling hurt and afraid once when a young child said she hated me simply because I wanted her to come inside as outdoor playtime was ending. When I asked myself why I was feeling offended from something a small child was saying to me, I realized that I was reacting as if I were a four-year-old instead of a thirty-two-year-old. I was able to regroup, remember my guidance role as her teacher, and, without taking what she said personally, scoop the girl up in my arms and say, "Ooh, I can hear some strong feelings from you. Right now we are all going inside."

Interviewing parents, siblings, and extended family members is another way to find out how emotional expression was perceived or accepted throughout the generations. For example, when I was in graduate school and taking a grief counseling course, we were asked to interview our parents about the ways they dealt with grief and loss. I flew home to Israel from the United States especially to ask my mother some questions about that. She described how when she lost someone or was sad, she immediately put on steel armor over her feelings—metaphorically speaking—straightened up, and made herself strong and very busy. I recognized much of myself in hearing her description. At the time, I needed to allow myself to acknowledge and grieve a serious loss of my own, and I did not understand what was holding me back. After our meeting and interview, I was able to let go of my own steel-like armor that I seemed to have inherited from her. I allowed myself a flood of emotion and healthy grief over a past loss I had denied myself from processing for many years prior.

Listening to family members tell their emotional memory stories can give us a clue into why or how our parents stressed some areas of behavior whereas others were less important to them. We begin to discover that not all their reactions were always about what we were doing. Very often their enormous anger was not about our deeds. Rather, it was about their fears or shame from their own early childhood experiences. Realizing this, we can see how it helps children if we acknowledge our mistakes or misplaced expressions of anger. It helps to validate their feelings of confusion that are a result of witnessing our feelings. If a child feels confused or does not understand why the adult is so angry, she will most likely take on the responsibility for the rage: she will feel that she is inherently bad even if from an adult's point of view it makes no sense. When we show that we know what our part was, we release the child from taking responsibility for our actions. We model taking responsibility for our own feelings and actions, and we allow the child a more realistic interpretation of the events.

Draw about it. Early in the morning, when preschool children arrived in my classroom in Israel, they found baskets of oil pastels and paper available on tables if they wanted to draw right away. Fresh from encounters with their dreams or confused by the antics and interactions with significant adults in their lives, they would find comfort in expression through the soft, fuzzy, magical colors and creative medium of pastels. I noticed one or two of the children sigh as they swirled and whirled the crayons, making shapes and forms rising out of their subconscious minds. Sometimes they knew what they wanted to draw right from the start; sometimes they found out as their drawing progressed. If they brought their creation to me, we talked about it. "Look at your picture and tell me what you see," I would say. As they chattered, I would guide and support their discovery, bearing witness to their tales of life, real and imagined. Sometimes I asked, "Do you like your picture?" And then, "Why?" or "Why not?" When the child had nothing further to say, I gave him a few choices: "You can hang it up, take it home, throw it away, give it to me. . . ." Whatever the children chose, I wanted to know why they made that decision. Mostly they knew why and told me right away. Sometimes they fell silent, and I would respect that too.

In the summer of 1987, I was invited to study in America. I was at the beginning of a sabbatical as a preschool and kindergarten teacher with the Ministry of Education in Israel. I was also nearing the end of a second failed marriage. Change was in the air for me. Huge, broad, windy strokes of change were swirling around my head, through my heart, and all around my life. Paradigms of self-loathing and feelings of unworthiness were starting to shift ever so slightly, but inside me it felt like the rumblings of an earthquake. At the time I was participating in a women's encounter group facilitated by a strong, insightful, and energetic woman who was also my tennis partner five mornings a week for many years. One day she brought out large pieces of paper and oil pastels and invited us to draw anything we liked. Feeling a bit intimidated, as I am no artist, and not knowing what or how to draw, I set about moving the crayons around the paper, timidly and cautiously at first. Before long I was sketching and drawing with full force, using every color possible from the large box of pastels.

When I had completed my drawing, I sat back and stared in surprise. I had drawn a huge, colorful bird with large, open eyes spreading its wings and flying out of a golden cage. The door of the cage was flung wide open, and the colorful bird was on its way out and up. I had not planned the picture. It had progressed spontaneously while I was drawing. Our group leader gasped as she noticed me staring at my picture. "You're leaving!" she exclaimed. The others gathered around, and we all looked intently at the picture I had created. I felt the earthquake rumbling somewhere deep inside me and looked up at them all. Their startled, supportive eyes gazed back at me. I held their gaze firmly and started nodding my head up and down. "Yes," I whispered, "I think I am." I left Israel for America less than a year later.

Sometimes when I awaken from my dreams, I think I should take out some oil pastels, just as the young children used to do so many years ago in my classroom, and draw out the shadows of my soul through the soft, fuzzy, magical colors. And then, instead, almost in a dream state, I stumble into my study, turn on the computer, and seek out my personal Web site. I sigh deeply as I "swirl and whirl" the keys, making shapes and forms out of my subconscious mind and memory—sometimes knowing what I want to say right from the start and, at other times, finding out as my writing progresses.

Now as a teacher educator I give this same exercise to students. They get to draw anything they like. Using a specific set of questions, similar to those I use with young children, I help the students talk about what they see in their pictures. They describe future plans, shattered dreams, long-lost childhood memories, poignant stories of losing and missing loved ones, and different ways they perceive themselves generally. Sometimes they cry. And one or two have had an epiphany that was helpful to their personal development. Many years after I taught a student, she wrote to me in an e-mail: "In one of the classes I took with you, you had the students bring in oil pastels and draw pictures. This was an incredible learning moment for me. I want to do that exercise with my co-workers at my internship, but I can't find the list of questions you asked after we all hung our pictures on the wall. . . . This would be a great exercise for my co-workers to learn from."

These are the kinds of things I usually say:

- Look at your picture and tell me what you see.
- Did you know that's what you wanted to draw when you began?
- When did you start to realize what you were going to draw?
- Look at [some part of the picture]. Tell us more about it.
- If those birds/flowers/trees/rocks/etc. were people, who would they be?
- Where are the people?
- Where are you in this picture?
- Look at your picture now. Do you like it?
- What do you or don't you like about it?
- If you could change anything, what would you do?
- When we are done you can hang it up, take it home, throw it away, or give it to me. What do you choose?
- Is there anything else you would like to tell us about what you see in your picture?
- Thank you for sharing your picture with us.

Naturally, I would add different, more specific questions in order to help each person explore his or her own picture more deeply. There are a few rules to the exercise. Students listening to the person describing a picture are not allowed to comment, cheer, applaud, or laugh. Their role is to be supporters and listeners. No one is forced to talk about a drawing. It is voluntary. Give the student (or yourself) enough time to think through an answer when you ask probing questions. Don't be afraid of the silence while they are thinking about what to say. And, finally, try not to make value judgments like "Good job! What a great artist you are!" "Oh, what a pretty picture! What bright colors!" "I see a car, tree, flower, house," etc. You were not in the mind and heart of the person as he or she made the drawing, and you cannot interpret the images or symbols the artist has created.

Get therapy. Researching the self is another way of thinking about therapy or counseling. I have participated in therapies of one kind or another for decades. Some counselors have been catalysts for meaningful self-alteration. Others were supportive but not necessarily effective as they accompanied me on my self-exploration journey. For example, it is important for me that a counselor has a sense of humor that matches my own because over the years laughter has been one thing that has helped me deal with life's challenges. Of course, counselors and therapists cannot perform miracles. They are not able to change anything unless a person is open and willing to explore, confront, and transform herself or himself.

I have always found that when a therapist is nonjudgmental and authentic with me, I am able to develop a trusting relationship. Once I feel emotionally safe, I uncover and share the uncomfortable aspects, vulnerabilities, or frailties of myself. Indeed, I have welcomed the opportunity to research and get to know myself even if it has sometimes felt uncomfortable or painful. It is almost as if each time I uncover pieces of myself that I was not aware of before I am meeting someone new and different. It becomes exciting to unravel the threads and realize connections between early childhood experiences and present attitudes, behaviors, or feelings.

Recently I received an e-mail from a colleague at work, a teacher educator like me. She wrote to me after having read my book *Confronting Our Discomfort*, where I suggest therapy as one way for teachers to understand their biases:

> 66 Interesting concept, including therapy as part of education training. Having a background in education and counseling, I have often reflected on how much my counseling background has helped me in my role as a teacher. It has also helped me tremendously in my personal life and my ability to communicate with the significant people in my life, especially my husband, which leads to a very strong marriage. I have often expressed to people that I think everyone would benefit from counseling and get strange reactions because they think they have to have major 'issues' to participate in the counseling process. However, I never thought about making it a requirement in teacher education training. 99

Read and study. Some people prefer to learn about themselves through reading books, attending workshops, or participating in support groups. I know that after I have read a book and years later read it again, I realize new and different things from the first time around. By the same token, when I reread some of my past journal entries, I am amazed at either how I have changed or, on the other hand, how much I have stayed the same!

I have found that when I think of this type of reflection as researching the self, it becomes less about whether I think I am emotionally healthy or not. All human beings have many different emotions and ways of expressing them. This is what makes us all diverse, complex, and interesting. There is nothing *weird* or *unhealthy* about wanting to understand ourselves better. I would go even one step further, and suggest that it is our *responsibility* to understand ourselves better if we are to be intentional in our interactions and relationships with children.

CONCLUSION

" I learned about performing very early in life. For from when I was eighteen months old, I learned ballet dancing with Elaine Archibald. Every day until I was ten or so I would attend ballet classes and appeared in concerts. I dreamed of becoming famous and dancing one day in Covent Garden. My mother would tell me about how I would become famous and she would sit in the special audience box and watch me dance. When I was ten, ballet dancing was taken away. Something about my being anemic or not having time to play. As I write this I have just realized why I was so emphatic with one of my students recently. She had described in class that until she had been involved in a car accident she had studied ballet and jazz dance. Now she was going into the teaching profession. I asked her if she was well enough to dance and she nodded her head vigorously, but said that she did not have the confidence any longer. I became quite excited and exclaimed vehemently that she must return to dancing and follow her heart. I went so far as to say that I hoped I could talk her out of teaching during the

semester and get her back into dancing. Hm . . . I wonder . . . was I really talking about myself? " (Personal
journal entry, January 2006)

Making connections between our early emotional memories
and the situations that cause us discomfort helps us to become
more intentional in our interactions. Researching the self is good
in and of itself. But it is my responsibility, especially as a teacher
of young children, to know why I do what I do. This makes me a
professional. I will be less liable to hurt or humiliate children in my
care when I make decisions and take action using both child development knowledge and self-understanding. This does not mean I
am not spontaneous. Nevertheless, in the beginning of my reflection
I might find myself behaving artificially, even stalling, in order to
work out which parts of my behavior rise up uncontrollably from
within me. As I become more used to communicating with myself
and negotiating these feelings with intentional behaviors, I become
more able to flow, "self-reflecting on my feet," as it were. Sometimes I find myself thinking, "Ah, there is that old anxiety coming
up to haunt me again. Welcome. What have you come to teach or
remind me today?" It might be right at the moment when a child
is having a tantrum, fighting with another child, or yelling curse
words at me.

When I was a young child, I would have a tantrum after long
periods of being very obedient and compliant. It was as if something snapped and I needed to break out of my goodness shell! My
mother would become very upset and admonish me, telling me
that I was destroying her and making my stepfather very angry.
Her anxiety about enraging my stepfather would stop me dead in
my tracks, and I would immediately take hold of myself and start

apologizing. Later, I would leave little notes around the house, apologizing profusely, begging forgiveness, or promising I would never be bad again. This pattern would repeat itself until I was a teenager. I do not remember my mother acknowledging the notes nor accepting my apology. I felt I was a very bad person—harmful, destructive, and causing everyone trouble. Those feelings stayed with me without respite or redemption until much later into my adult years, when I was finally able to uncover them with my therapist.

To this day, I am extra patient and forgiving with children who have tantrums. I do everything I can to assist them as they work through the pain and humiliation of that experience. It is as if I try to redeem myself through them over and over again. I look into the child's eyes as he or she expresses torment, fear, and confusion during a tantrum, and reflected in those eyes see myself, or what some people call "my inner child" (Bradshaw 1990). On the one hand, this has made me unafraid and effective in helping children in these situations. For example, when I was director of our university child care center, teachers would call on me to help them out with the children who were having tantrums. On the other hand, at times I am not effective at all because I find myself overcompensating for my own painful memories. In the next chapter, I will discuss my strategies for helping children get through their tantrums. I will remind you that I am only able to suggest what to do based on my own childhood survival skills and life experience. What I do might not work for you!

It is not important *how* each one of us chooses to take on this type of self-reflection. It is, however, important that we *do* take it on at all. John Bradshaw warns us that if we choose not to resolve our own unresolved issues from the past, we are liable to violate a child's sense of self.

" I consider anything that violates a person's sense of self
to be violence. . . . In my definition, violence occurs when
a more powerful and knowledgeable person destroys the
freedom of a less powerful person for whom he or she is
significant. It goes without saying that it is violent to choose
to bring children into the world and incest [*sic*], batter,
torture, imprison, starve, or morally corrupt them. Other
forms of violence are not as obvious. It is violent to choose
to bring children into the world and:

- Desert them *emotionally* . . .
- Refuse to set limits . . .
- Use them as a scapegoat for your anger and shame
- Refuse to resolve your own unresolved issues from the
  past. " (Bradshaw 1992, 44, 46)

It becomes our responsibility that at the same time we consider
how to best guide and facilitate children's social emotional development, we work at resolving our own emotional issues as well.

References

Bradshaw, J. 1990. *Homecoming: Reclaiming and championing
your inner child.* New York: Bantam Books.

———. 1992. *Creating love: The next great stage of growth.* New
York: Bantam Books.

Eliot, T. S. Little Gidding. In *Four quartets.* New York: Harcourt,
Brace, 1943.

Jacobson, T. 2003. *Confronting our discomfort: Clearing the way
for anti-bias in early childhood.* Portsmouth, N.H.: Heinemann.

Jones, M., and M. Shelton. 2006. *Developing your portfolio: Enhancing your learning and showing your stuff.* New York: Routledge, Taylor and Francis Group.

Leavitt, R. L. 1994. *Power and emotion in infant-toddler day care.* Albany: State University of New York Press.

Lerner, H. 2004. *The dance of fear: Rising above anxiety, fear, and shame to be your best and bravest self.* New York: HarperCollins.

Miller, A. 2001. *The truth will set you free: Overcoming emotional blindness and finding your true adult self.* New York: Basic Books.

Posner, G. 2005. *Field experience: A guide to reflective teaching.* Boston: Pearson.

CHAPTER SIX

WE USE DISCIPLINE, NOT PUNISHMENT

You don't have to hurt me to teach me.

—SABRINA, UNDERGRADUATE STUDENT

We need a kiss a day.

—ANGELIQUE KIDJO

As I was driving to work yesterday, listening to music and looking at the glorious colors of autumn leaves along the roadside, I suddenly had an overwhelming understanding of what it is to be an adult. Released from blaming others, free of anger, I felt master of my domain, in charge of my choices, and aware that my attitude or how I feel is up to me and *only* me. No one can make me feel thus, such, or any other way. I can choose to feel bad, worthless, undeserving, pathetic, a victim. Or I can choose to feel that I am A-OK, a human with frailties, weaknesses, and (yes!) strengths too. Indeed, I am responsible for my actions, feelings, and thoughts. No one can make me do or feel anything without my permission. At the same time, I realized that with the privilege of these choices about attitude comes an awesome responsibility: to do good; to be kind, forgiving, understanding, and compassionate to others. This is our responsibility just because we are all human, celebrating the joy and sorrows of humankind—just because we are all connected.

When I act as a responsible adult, there is meaning and purpose to my life, and I feel worthwhile. It occurs to me that discipline is all about learning this awesome responsibility. We must wrap boundaries of compassion around our youngest children, so that they might learn to feel worthwhile in this way themselves, forever and ever. Don't get me wrong—boundaries of compassion are not wishy-washy or weak. They are firm and serious. They stop you in your tracks and hold you tight in their embrace. They mean business, and they repeat themselves over and over again until you get it! They don't neglect or ignore you. They are relentless, constant, consistent, and strong, and they accompany you wherever you go. They show you how deeply we care about you. Compassion is deep and wide. Our youngest children, and most likely also our own inner child, need buckets, tubs-full, rivers, mountains of it.

WE KEEP CHILDREN SAFE AND FEELING LOVED
EVEN IN THE MOST TRYING SITUATIONS.

Teaching without Hurting

Children love their mamas and papas. So why do we hurt children
to teach them? For example, when they are very young, and they
learn to curse by imitating the group of adults they adore, why do
we wash their mouths out with soap, put pepper on their tongues,
or inflict other such punishment? Why can't we, instead, hold
young children close and seriously, earnestly, tell them that we love
them and that when they use those curse words, it makes us all feel
unsafe? Young children need adults for their survival. They need
us to approve of and love them, to guide them with kindness and
compassion so that they will grow to be humane. Thinking of those
innocent, trusting, yearning, curious, mischievous, needy eyes, I
wonder why we hurt children to teach them.

Discipline versus Punishment

The root of the word "discipline" comes from the Latin word
disciplina, which means teaching or learning, and from *discipu-
lus,* which means pupil. When I look at the word "discipline" it
reminds me of "disciple"—a follower who is guided by a mentor.
Many great teachers throughout the ages spring to my mind when
I think of disciples. Whether they are biblical or historical figures,
mythical or real, their characteristics seem the same to me. Namely,
teachers of disciples are kind but firm. Their method of teaching is

through metaphors, allegories, and stories and mostly through setting an example. They are forgiving and nonjudgmental. They give clear messages about what they think, believe, and feel. What do you think of when you hear the word "disciple"? Do you think of punitive masters or forgiving teachers?

Do you remember some of the things people recalled when asked to think of how they were disciplined when they were young? Beatings, spankings, kneeling on rice; being yelled at; having their mouths washed out with soap; or suffering humiliation from pinching, hair pulling, or name calling: those were disciplinary methods that people said were abusive. I term those types of actions "punishment," because I think of discipline as something different: something that is clear, firm, and loving—that is caring, guiding, and predominantly about relationships. Discipline is important for young children. It steers them toward living successfully in an adult society. It guides them in becoming critical-thinking, self-regulated citizens of the world. Discipline is respectful. Children feel safe when they are disciplined. When they are punished, on the other hand, they become fearful, defensive, resentful, and anxious.

When we think of discipline and young children, most of us filter our knowledge of child development and appropriate practice through our own early childhood experiences and memories of punishments received or witnessed. That is why, when I ask adults to share ways they were disciplined, they usually reply with a list of punishments. David Elkind describes the difference between the two:

> " One idea of childrearing and discipline is instructive; it is a matter of teaching children social skills and attitudes. The other conception of childrearing and discipline is punitive, a matter of stamping out misbehavior through punishment.

The difference in our starting out conceptions of discipline is important because it determines how we look at, and treat, what we as adults label misbehavior. *"*   (Elkind 2007)

We become confused between punishment—"Sit in the corner facing the wall until you can be good!"—and discipline—"In our class I want everyone to be safe here. When you threaten someone with throwing a block at them, no one is safe." Many years ago when I was director of a large campus child care center, I gave the teaching staff a holiday gift of a little book with some wise and humorous instructions for early childhood teachers. One of the instructions says, "Punishment is for criminals, guidance is for children" (Raines 1995). I like to think of discipline as *guidance*.

Children Are Powerless

From the moment children are born, adults are in charge, telling them what to do when, how to dress, what to eat and how much to eat, and what and how to feel. For example, we line children up and tell them when they are allowed to go to the bathroom. We make major life decisions for them as part of our own actions of divorcing, remarrying, bringing siblings into their lives, or moving to new towns, countries, continents, and schools. We hardly ever ask or allow them to tell us how they feel about any of these situations. We yell at them, insult and humiliate them, and intrude on their emotional and physical space without asking their permission or even warning them. For example, instead of kneeling down at eye level in front of a small child, explaining that we are about to wipe her nose, we come from behind and thrust the tissue in her face, often startling or shocking the child to tears. And then we say things like, "Why are you crying? We have to clean your nose!"

Adults monitor the choice of curriculum materials, colors of paints, or length of time children spend in each play center. Just as children become involved in a project or assignment, we demand that they move on to another play center. We determine when they rise in the morning and go to school. We are usually in a rush and force them to fit into our pace and schedule. The environment, including furniture, toilet seats, technology equipment, and even the height of light switches, is usually organized to fit in with adult needs. If children feel frustrated or anxious, sad or grieving, we force them to sing out loud, clap their hands, and put a smile on their face. When they cry, we tell them to swallow their tears or we will give them something "real" to cry about. When they laugh, we warn them, "It will end in tears!"

Young children are powerless. Therefore, it is only natural that they develop ways to feel in control of their lives. I often compare children to oppressed peoples because of the similar ways they reach for control—through creating coalitions and instigating small acting-out revolutions or by becoming aggressive, apathetic, or ma-nipulating. Some lose themselves in fantasy. Others develop ways to control *us*. For example, many years ago my neighbor's child would hold her food in her mouth for a long time without swallowing it. She would sit in her high chair, cheeks puffed out with the food, and watch as her mother became hysterical with worry, frustration, and rage. I have known many children who did not participate in activities. They sat, their bodies becoming too heavy for teachers to move, and refused to join in at circle, during free play, or even snacktime. Like my neighbor's child, they seemed to be observing patiently while the adults around them became helpless with con-cern, not knowing how to budge the child from his place and un-able to force him into participation. And then, sometimes it seems that there are other ways children control adults by when, how, or if they choose to become potty trained or go to the bathroom.

When children feel unloved or unwanted for one reason or another, they seek our attention. Achieving the type of attention they deserve is elusive to them. They have no control over their parents' or guardians' priorities or life challenges. But they still need consistent, unconditional, and supportive loving. This is yet another area where children may develop ways to gain control over their lives. Attention seeking can take on many different forms, and often it is through negative or self-destructive behaviors. When teachers tell me, "He's just doing that [whatever it is] for attention," my reply is usually something like, "Then find many constructive ways to give him attention! If he is doing those other unacceptable-to-you types of things for attention, he still needs attention!" It is at those very moments when children need our attention that I see teachers choosing to ignore them as an effective strategy. In other words, we take away from them what they need so desperately from us. It is difficult for children to feel worthwhile or develop a solid, healthy self-identity when they are made to feel helpless, neglected, or excluded.

I Want Everyone to Be Safe Here

In order to guide young children effectively, we must understand the difference between punishment and discipline. It is important to remember that children feel little control over their lives. Setting strong and consistent boundaries for children is the most loving form of guidance we can facilitate. It teaches them responsibility and self-regulation. More than that, it shows them we care about their well-being and future. A neglectful, hands-off attitude when we ignore children's behaviors or actions is as destructive for children as beating them or forcing them to kneel on rice. Both are disrespectful.

Discipline is crucial in developing democratic citizens. In a democratic society we negotiate our freedoms and do not intrude on each other's personal space without permission. We create laws and rules that are dynamic and open to the changing times and needs of the citizens in our communities. We recognize free speech as a basic human right. And at the same time, we ensure that speech will not endanger, insult, humiliate, offend, or hurt others. We learn to take responsibility for our actions or face the consequences.

The early childhood classroom is sometimes the young child's first encounter with a community of her peers. Here she will learn to negotiate her freedom in relation to others and learn how not to intrude in their personal space. You, the teacher and the leader of the classroom community, will want to model those interactions with utmost respect. Children are constantly watching, listening, and imitating significant adults in their lives, for this is the way they learn.

In my classroom I have one rule: *I want everyone to be safe here.* Everything we do or say as children, teachers, and parents is measured against that rule. Some things are negotiable or open for debate. Others are never acceptable. For example, it is never good for anyone if any of us, teachers included, hurts or humiliates another person. We must all be able to express how we feel—but not if our words create a hostile or unsafe space for others in our classroom community. In order for everyone to be safe here, we have community discussions so that we might learn what people are feeling and thinking about. We develop guidelines for how to speak to one another respectfully so that everyone will feel heard safely.

As the leader of a classroom community, the teacher has the last word. In the final analysis it is always his or her responsibility to care for and educate children. Nevertheless, children are allowed to express their feelings, register complaints, make suggestions, share their ideas, and contribute to the resolution of problems.

Recently I was having dinner with colleagues. During the course of our conversation, my friend was telling me how she and her husband were planning to take their son on a trip out of the country when he graduated from high school. She was pondering out loud to me about which continent to visit and asked for my opinion because I have lived in Africa, the Middle East, Europe, and the United States. I asked her where her son would like to go. She became speechless for a moment and then started to laugh. "I never thought of that," she said, shaking her head from side to side. "Ask him," I suggested. "You don't have to go wherever he wants, but you can find out what he thinks about it before you all decide together." My colleague seemed grateful for my suggestion.

Young children have ideas too. Just ask them! You don't have to do whatever they want, but you can find out what they think about it before you all decide together—and sometimes you will have to make the final decision all by yourself!

It works with parents too. As a teacher in the classroom and while director of the campus child care center, I always initiated some type of parent advisory committee. A group of volunteer parents met with me on a monthly basis to discuss any concerns or questions they had. Sometimes they would bring questions from parents who did not participate on the committee, and in that way they would act as representatives for all the parents. We would talk about everything and anything from safety and nutrition to curriculum and discipline. I would make a written note of each concern or question they had. Some of them I could answer then and there. At other times, I would have to research and get back to them later with an answer. Some of their suggestions were good for the children of the center. Others were not developmentally appropriate or might not be suitable for the other families.

As the professional, I would weigh which suggestions I could put into effect and which I would have to refuse. I took parents' concerns and suggestions seriously and would bring them to the attention of the teachers at our professional development meetings or to my aide during the years when I was a classroom teacher. If I thought suggestions were inappropriate, I would explain why, always supporting my explanations with current articles, the latest research, or information from colleagues in the field. Once, the parents wanted the center to provide organic food for the children. While it was healthy and undoubtedly more nutritious for them, it was too costly for the budget at the time. We would have had to raise tuition fees significantly, and many parents would not have been able to afford them. But I still wrote down the suggestion, researched it seriously, and followed up with detailed reasons about my final decision. At other times, the parents may have wanted me to use forms of punishment or types of curriculum that I knew were inappropriate for young children. I would hear them out and then patiently explain why it was not developmentally appropriate, usually supporting my responses with current information from the field.

I realized at one time that I had been giving out too many articles. This happened when a parent complained to our program coordinator that the faucets in the restrooms were not turning on properly. The program coordinator told the parent she would let me know about the faucets, and the parent exclaimed, "Oh no! Please don't tell Tamar. She will just give me another article to read!" Most of the time, though, parents were pleased with our interactions. They felt heard, and they understood the boundaries. They learned to trust my professional judgment as long as I continued to treat their concerns and questions seriously and respectfully. At the same time, I was able to keep my finger on the pulse of how parents were feeling about the care and education their children were receiving.

There are many instances when I hear teachers say to young children, "That's not nice." They might be referring to hitting another child, spitting, biting, pushing, kicking, or cursing. There are a variety of behaviors or reactions that seem to conjure up that expression from teachers. Yet hitting, cursing, or any such behaviors have nothing to do with whether they are "nice" or not. The issue is about safety. If we are honest with ourselves, we might admit that it probably feels quite satisfying for a child to blurt out a curse word or punch someone in the nose when she is angry or frustrated. It might feel quite "nice," thank you! At times like these, what is relevant to say is, "That is not *safe*. I want everyone to be safe here." This provides an opportunity to remind children that even when we are angry or upset, we are not allowed to hurt other people. In addition, each time I say the words, "I want everyone to be safe here," I remind *myself* about the rule and realize that those words apply to me too. We can never say it too many times. Both children and adults learn through repetition.

It's Good to Call Children by Their Real Names

One of the directors of a child care center in Texas recently told me that she used to call children "Pumpkin" and other such pet names, until one day four-year-old Chanede looked her straight in the eye and said indignantly, "I ain't your punkin!"

I have always been averse to treating children as if they are cute little pets, feeding their minds with bunnies and balloons, bears and other silly, smiling animals, as if that is all their brains

will understand. "Call children by their real names," I always tell
teachers. "Don't trivialize children. When they run up to tell you
a story, don't say, 'How sweet or funny' or laugh out loud at their
'cuteness.' Share real art, challenging and intellectual ideas with
children, and treat them with respect, as you would a guest in your
house." Always included in my teachings is a reminder to call children by their names. Indeed, I take great pains to find out how all
people like to be addressed, and to pronounce their names exactly
as they would like. Is it Katherine or Kate? Rebecca or Bekah? Eliz-
abeth, Meg, or Beth? Robert or Bob or maybe Rob? Daniel, Danny,
or Dan? Thomas or Tom? James or Jim? Jenny or Nian?

> " Many of the Asian students and parents I have encountered
> change their birth names and those of their children to
> American ones. They tell me it is in consideration of Ameri-
> cans, it is easier to pronounce. I understand how they feel in
> some ways. Hardly anyone spells or pronounces my name
> correctly. Somehow an extra "a" is added to the end of my
> name: Tamar—Tamara. What's in a name? However, names
> are given at birth and for many of us our name has signifi-
> cance and is part of our identity. For example, 1949 was one
> year after the creation of the State of Israel when I was born
> in Southern Rhodesia. My father wanted to call me Dolores
> but my mother did not want my name to remind me of 'sor-
> row.' And so they chose a Hebrew name because they were
> excited about the promise of a newly formed Jewish State.
> They chose excitement and promise for me rather than sor-
> row. I think of that sometimes. When people add an 'a' to
> the end of Tamar, it becomes a Russian or an American

name, depending on the pronunciation. Learning the correct pronunciation of someone's birth name shows respect for people from different cultures. " (Jacobson 2003, 14–15)

When I was a child, I loved it when my father would call me "Tamarika." It felt soft, gentle, dear, and special. It came from his culture that I yearned to be a part of. He spoke to my stepmother in Ladino, a language I could not understand. I have often wondered why he did not teach me Ladino and why I never sought to learn it. When he would say "Tamarika," I immediately felt connected to something that felt deep and important to my roots, his roots—a space where I, too, could belong for a moment. I would beam from somewhere deep inside myself and feel a pleasurable gurgle in my throat, almost like a purr.

Pleasure is such a personal, associative feeling. "Punkin" did not do it for Chanede, but "Tamarika" surely felt good to me. I still think it is a good thing to call children by their names. If you really, really feel a great urge to use an endearment term of your own choosing, just ask children for their permission first—that's all. Children know what they want. They will tell you, if you take the time to hear.

Suggested Strategies

The discipline strategies that have worked for me are connected to life experiences, early emotional memories, and acquired knowledge along the way. I choose to share them here with you with the understanding that some might not suit your temperament or make sense in relation to your life experiences.

Carry Children on Your Back

I like to carry children on my back. I most probably experienced this growing up in Africa by riding on my nanny's back as a child. Once I read about the lives of chimpanzees, the closest mammals to humankind, and discovered that they are well-adjusted because their young are carried on their mother's bodies (Goodall 2006). This information supported what I had already experienced in my early years growing up in Africa, not only with my own nanny but also from witnessing others. In fact, when my son was a young child, it felt natural and appropriate for me to carry him on my back, sometimes even as far as a couple of miles or so to and from the center of our town to our home. The only reason I stopped was because he became too heavy for my body to support him at around age six or seven.

When I was a preschool and kindergarten teacher in Israel, I worked in a one-room school house and was responsible for thirty-five children ages two and a half through five years, with one aide to assist me. I carried children on my back for a variety of reasons. If a child was crying, I would scoop him up onto my back. It was most effective. The proximity to my body was immediately soothing, and I still had my hands free to work with the other children who needed me. Second, if there was a child who was biting the other children, the perfect place for her was on my back. That way, I knew where she was and could help her stop the behavior in a firm but loving way. Now, you are probably thinking that all the children must have started biting in the hope that they would be rewarded by riding on my back, right? Well, let me assure you, that never happened. Most of the time the child did not want to be on my back. She wanted to be down playing and interacting with her classmates. In addition, the other children were usually too busy playing or working to be bothered with who was on my back or not. Each time I scooped up a child onto my back I would say something like, "I want everyone to be safe here. Come and be with me until you are safe again and can stop biting (punching, hitting, running away, etc.)."

When I became director of the campus child care center, it took a few years before the teachers felt comfortable with the idea of carrying children on their backs. Finally, a few of them found it helpful. They did not agree to place the children directly on their backs. So we bought backpacks. A few years ago, I received a letter from one of the parents preparing to send a child to kindergarten after being at our center for four years. The parent wrote:

" We brought [our daughter] to [your center], a scared and shy toddler, who preferred the company of teachers to children. I can remember how I would sneak in at the end of the day hoping to find [my child] playing happily with some of the children. But, a lump would grow in my throat when I would instead find her riding safely in the pack on the back of 'friend teacher Pat' (that's what [my daughter] called her). Looking back, I am extremely grateful for the patience and understanding that was afforded her during her first months at the center. . . . Thanks for taking such great care of our precious one. "

Most teachers I know would never dream of carrying children on their backs. "Friend teacher Pat" must have thought it could work for her even though she did not have the same early childhood experiences as mine. It made sense to her and felt useful. She became comfortable using that strategy. I always remember the

day, soon after I first came to the campus child care center, when
I walked into the infant room and saw an older infant crying by
the gate. I noticed that the teacher was busy diapering another
infant. She called out to the crying child, "I'm coming, I'm coming." I turned to the teacher and said, "Why don't you put her on
your back?" She looked at me, alarmed. "I don't put children on
my back," she replied. I caught myself in a moment of bias. Growing up in Africa, I had just assumed that all brown-skinned people
carry their children on their backs, just as my nanny had done with
me. The teacher in the infant room whom I had spoken to was
an African American woman. When I shared with her my biased
assumption, she generously laughed out loud at my folly. She reminded me that although she was African American, she was not
African, and she had never in her life transported a child on her
back. In the end, though, she was prepared to learn my "different"
method. Many years later I caught sight of her carrying a crying
toddler on her back in a backpack.

Choose Your Battles

Keep things clear, firm, and simple without long, preachy sentences
of explanation. Some things are simply not safe. Other battles will
depend on your own personal bottom line, which, in turn, will depend on your own fears, values, beliefs, and early childhood memories. What can you tolerate? What is important to you? Each of us
has a different tolerance level. For example, I never cared what my
son wore to school. I allowed him to choose his clothes from a very
young age, and believe me—some of his outfits were quite amazing!
On the other hand, I was clear and firm about his bedtime. He had
to be in bed by 7:00 PM—no ifs, ands, or buts! Some teachers will
not read a story to young children unless they are sitting straight up

with legs crossed. I do not mind if they lie on their tummies, lean to one side, or sit on their haunches. It seems that I have not changed my opinion about this. Just the other day, I noticed that some of the undergraduate students in my class had their feet propped up on chairs or were sprawled across the tables as we were discussing some topic or other like gender bias and the pros and cons of an all-girls school. I imagined how offended some of my professor colleagues would be if students sat like that in their class.

What is your bottom line? Which behaviors are more tolerable to you than others? Why? How would you identify what is important for you with regard to young children's behaviors or manners?

Follow Through

Follow through immediately, firmly, and clearly. So many teachers call across the room, "Sammy. Put that block down. How many times have I told you . . . ?" Calling across the room in that manner is almost as good as a dare. If you mean it, do it. In other words, physically go over to the child in question. Immediately, kneel down at the child's eye level, hold his hand that has the block in it, and say firmly, "I want everyone to be safe here. Throwing that block is not safe for anyone." Personally, I have never found that counting to three or calling out "How many times must I tell you?" are effective ways to stop a child from doing something dangerous. Following through is immediate and explicit. The message is right here and now—physically and verbally.

Mean What You Say

When I say that we are going to clean up the classroom before we go outside, I mean it! No ifs, ands, or buts! When a child starts running away from completing her chore, I scoop her up onto my back, and off we go together to finish cleaning up. On our way she might be squirming and trying to get down. I hold on tight and say, "It's time to clean up, and we all have to finish our chores before we can go out to play." The child is cleaning up along with me, as a part of my body. If I mean what I say, I must participate with enthusiasm. When I point to the puzzles and say, "Clean those up!" I am ordering, demanding, and commanding. When we gather the pieces together, I am participating and showing that I really mean it. I so badly want us to clean up everything that I am prepared to do it, to get it done together. I do not go about completing paperwork or doing something different if I really want the room cleaned up. I have found, over the years, that most of what children learn from me is through my example. If I mean what I say, there is a tone in my voice that is clear, confident, and sure. I do not need to yell or give what some people call "the [angry, scary] *look*."

We give children a confusing message when asking them if they want to do something that we are going to do anyway. For example, if we are intending to read a story at circle time and we ask children if they *want* to hear a story, some of them might call out in reply, "No!" If reading a story really is an option, then asking them has meaning. Be clear about what you are going to do. If there is not an option, state the plan clearly and simply: "We are going to read a story now." Meaning what we say depends on knowing what we mean to begin with. I find that when I am clear with myself first, I will be more effective in meaning what I say.

Tell children what they can do. For example, if they jump on the furniture, pick them up and, as you stand them back on the floor, say, "Jump on the floor." Be explicit, even when you praise them. Make it relevant to what they are doing and not to your opinion about them. "I see you have placed enough plates and cups on the table for everyone. We are ready for lunch now!" instead of "Good job! I like the way you set the table."

Time-Out Is for Teachers

" When used as discipline, the time-out is one of a group of techniques—including the name-on-the-board, an assigned yellow or red 'light,' and the disciplinary referral slip—that still rely on blame and shame to bring a child's behavior 'back into line.' One of the problems with these techniques, seen by some adults as 'logical consequences,' is that generally they are more logical to the adult than to the child. Although the adult's intent is to discipline rather than punish, children tend to perceive these traditional discipline techniques as 'the infliction of pain and suffering,' which is, in fact, a fairly standard definition of punishment. "
(Gartrell 2004, 64)

I will most certainly take a child out of a situation where he might hurt himself or others. Even if he is kicking and screaming and does not want to leave the area in question, I say quietly and firmly, "I want everyone to be safe here, and so I must take you out of this area now until I can help you become safe again." But I will not abandon the child on a chair alone, in a reading corner, in a "thinking chair," or in any other such place. I might take the child for a short walk outside the classroom where we can talk together or even just be together in silence for a while. I might put him on my back or hold him in my arms as we talk through what has happened. I do not send the child, as a distraction, to help set the table for lunch. There should be no distractions. I will relate to the child then and there about what is happening with him. Time-out is for taking a deep breath together and reinforcing classroom community rules. It is not the time for abandonment or exclusion.

Over the years, time and again, I have interviewed young children I see sitting in different types of special "thinking" chairs or time-out corners. Without exception they seem to have absolutely no idea why they are sitting there, and in some cases they tell me that they are in time-out because someone else hurt them. I prefer to think of time-out as being for teachers. When we are feeling overwhelmed or at the end of our rope, or if we think that we have run out of solutions and answers to problems, it is time for a time-out. It is a good time to say to the aide or coteacher, "I have to go out of the room for a moment. Please take over for me. I'll be back very soon." And then take a short walk, breathe deeply, wash your face, drink some water, and reflect on what has happened up to that moment. Sometimes, after a brief reprieve from a difficult situation, I have returned to the classroom and solved the problem instantly. Teachers certainly need time-out alone sometimes. Children need to be accompanied through theirs. I will address this again when I discuss children and tantrums.

Give Relevant Consequences

If you give consequences, make them relevant to the behavior. For example, in my classroom, if a child hits another, the consequence is that the child who hit is immediately expected to help me heal the hurt child. Relevant consequences that are connected to the behaviors are not always simple to work out. It might help to think of some of the things that happen on a daily basis and plan consequences ahead of time. That way you will be caught unawares less frequently and will not be blindsided by surprises. Mostly the consequences will include the teacher accompanying the child in her activity. For example, I take the child with me to heal the other one who has been hurt. We might need to find a Band-Aid and bring a glass of water or a tissue to dry the child's eyes, and we might just sit together and ask how the hurt child is feeling. Or if a child refuses to clean up, she and I will have to stay together in the room until her chore is completed before she can go outside. If I notice that she is staying inside too often, using the clean-up as an excuse to be with me, I make a note that the child might be seeking some attention—alone time with me. I think of other ways we can do things together that do not include hanging back to clean up. I would probably include her in a conversation about this: "I see that you like staying back in the classroom to clean up with me. But now it is time to be outside. Let's think of other ways we can do things together."

Make Wise Curriculum Choices

Education is not only about entertainment—fun is a side benefit. Curriculum should be interesting, relevant to children's experience, and challenging. When children are engaged, they become capable of achievement. Not only does this build self-esteem, for with a sense of accomplishment and achievement we feel worthwhile, but it also creates less opportunity for inappropriate behaviors. Children are natural researchers. They love to find out how or why things work, and they ask a lot of questions. They deserve curriculum that is rich in academic integrity so that they can expand their minds and brains. If we continuously give young children meaningless or petty tasks that are too easy and boring, or if we use inappropriate curriculum that is too difficult and abstract, we are going to double the instances of what teachers label "behavior problems."

One of my undergraduate students wrote journal entries about a four-year-old child she was observing. This child was reacting to unchallenging curriculum and, as a result, was being disciplined for her behavior by the teacher (the name of the child has been changed for confidentiality):

> " For example, Leslie was singing to herself during circle time one day and was not at all focused on going over the calendar and the weather of the day. The teacher decided to remove her from the circle until she could focus better; however, pulling her out of the group only gave her more privacy and did not at all hinder her from continuing her song.
>
> Today Leslie broke my heart. She was singing to herself during circle time and did not recite the date with the rest of the class. Ms. H. made Leslie recite it alone. Leslie barely squeaked the words out and Ms. H. kept yelling at her to use her 'big girl' voice. I was horrified. What's the big deal? They're 4, you can't control their every movement! Leslie was in tears by the time she got through the date. I was mortified. Her attention remained unfocused all day, even when she was removed from circle she did not face the class and kept singing. "

Recently I read an article in the *New York Times* about new studies that might "prompt a reassessment of the possible causes of disruptive behaviors in some children" (Carey 2007). Although, previously, professionals were afraid that children who were behaviorally challenged did not succeed academically in the higher grades, a couple of studies found that there was less need for concern. For example, one of the studies found that young children who were identified with behavior problems seemed to be as successful academically as their peers in grade school after all. The director of the Georgetown University Center on Health and Education, Sharon Landesman Ramey, was quoted in the article: "I think these may become landmark findings, forcing us to ask whether these acting out problems are secondary to the inappropriate maturity expectations that some educators place on young children as soon as they enter classrooms."

The Punching Cushion

" Deer Tamar,

My favorite thing we ever did together was take a big cushion and painting a face on it and imagining hitting it. I will always remember doing that with you. Thank you for being so good. Louv M. "

(A card received from a child when she left the center to go to kindergarten)

More than thirty years ago, when I was a young teacher in Israel, I took a course in bioenergetics. I learned where all our points of energy are situated and about how we store up energy in certain parts of our bodies. Our teacher, Rafi Rozen, was a dynamic man in his late sixties who was as vital and energetic as any person I have ever encountered. Among the many activities I learned from him about releasing energy was using the punching cushion. He taught us that pushing our arms back and forth in a punching motion was a primal way of releasing energy. He compared it to the way infants flail their arms up and back.

After learning about this, I created a punching cushion, similar to one that we had used in those bioenergetics classes, and I used it all the years I was a teacher of young children. It was very large and thick, so that when little hands punched it, they would not be hurt by hitting deep into the cushion while it was on the floor. I had very strict rules about how to use the cushion, and I would teach the children in groups before it was placed in the classroom as one of the activity centers. The rules were as follows:

- You may not punch the cushion alone. A teacher must be present with you. If you want to punch the cushion, please tell a teacher to come and be with you.
- You may not kick or throw the cushion around. You may only punch it with your fists. Only one person may punch the pillow at a time.
- I want everyone to be safe here. Therefore, you may never punch a person. Only the cushion.

Sitting next to the cushion, I accompanied the child as she punched it. Other children were allowed to come and join in by sitting and watching. First, I demonstrated to the child how to make a fist and punch, using strong motions with the arms back and forth into the pillow. Then I sat back quietly while the child punched. I made no comments like, "Oh, good job! What an excellent puncher you are!" or anything of that nature. Nevertheless, I watched and listened intently, making sure the child knew I was present and was concentrating on her actions. At times, children would say things while they were punching, like "I hate you!" or "I can punch and punch and punch!" Again, I made no comment. I did not say, "That's not a nice thing to say," or "Yes, you can punch and punch and punch." I was silent but present. Now and again the child would stop punching and look toward me. Then, I would say, "Are you done?" If she was not, she would be allowed to continue until deciding it was enough. At the end of the punching I would hold the child in my arms, rocking back and forth. During the punching exercise, the child released a lot of energy, which was both exciting and a little scary. Holding and rocking soothed and calmed the child. It also physically demonstrated to the child that she was safe and acceptable.

If, during the course of the exercise, I noticed that some of the things the child was saying needed my attention, I made a note to find out more later—at a different time—from the child and also, perhaps, from the parents or guardians. I was alert and attentive throughout. No doubt about it, I discovered instances of child abuse through some of the things children said as they punched. Mostly, though, their complaints were more about things like not being allowed to watch television or wear their favorite shirt or dress to school. These complaints seem small to adults. To children, these can seem like major issues, connected to their feeling that everything is out of their control and always being decided for them. These things make them mad! Oftentimes children did not say anything while punching the cushion. And that was all right too. We do not always have to know what children are thinking and feeling. But we can still accompany them while bearing witness to their punching exercise, being there to listen in silence.

Over time, children would come and ask for the cushion when they felt they needed it. It was not used in place of hitting children. In other words, if a child was pushing or hitting someone else, I would not rush to bring the pillow as a replacement activity or distraction for that behavior. I would deal with that in the usual, "I want everyone to be safe" way. But sometimes, in a way designed to feel spontaneous, I would invite a group of children to come with me to punch the cushion. They would watch and listen while each child had a turn punching.

They did not have to engage in the activity if they did not want to. Usually they would stay to watch and listen if they decided not to punch the cushion. In that way, it became a support group activity. This was a good way for the girls to muster up the courage to engage with the cushion. Many girls are fearful of expressing aggression, as they are taught early on that aggression is only for boys. With other children sitting close by to support the activity, girls seemed to allow themselves to participate in the punching. I often wonder what girls can do about their anger if they are never allowed to express it. And then I remember the ways I have always dealt with mine: through migraines, crying, or a sore stomach. Later in life I found that playing a strong game of tennis or taking a long, brisk walk was a great way to get my anger out. The punching cushion exercise is like that for young children—an appropriate way to express any and all types of feelings, especially anger or frustration!

I could tell many stories about how this exercise helped children in my classes. They could probably fill a whole separate book! But I always remember a three-year-old boy in one of my classes. "Chris" came from a loving family who gave him a lot of attention. They read to him, took him on outings, and all in all enjoyed his presence in their lives. When he turned three, his baby brother was born. Although the family did all the right things to make Chris still feel loved and included, he had a hard time accepting the new baby. His difficulties manifested themselves in the classroom: whenever he came to school, he was agitated and anxious. He would scratch the other children at every opportunity. His mother and I would make sure his nails were cut, and we talked about how to help him through this difficult time. Whenever I would call a group over to the punching pillow, Chris would be the first to come. He loved to punch. One day, he arrived at school, walked through the classroom door, threw down his coat, and called out to me, waving his hand in the air, "Bring me the cushion!" I raced over to him with it, and he punched and punched with all his might, over and over again. At the end, he lay in my arms as limp as could be while I rocked him back and forth. And then, suddenly, he sat up straight and looked up at me with a broad smile on his face. He said, "I love this school!" He had a peaceful day after that, interacting with the other children, cooperating, and playing.

Tantrums

" Dear Dr. Jacobson,

Thank you for your . . . presentation at the conference. It made me reflect on my beliefs about discipline and how I uphold those beliefs as a parent and as a program director. It gave me the strength to be there for my 3-year-old as she screamed and kicked and bit earlier today. It felt wonderful when my daughter finally accepted my embrace and melted into me. If I hadn't been at your presentation yesterday, I probably would have gotten angry and left her alone. . . . THANK YOU! "

(An e-mail letter from an attendee at one of my workshops about discipline, 2006)

To this day, I can remember what it felt like when I had a tantrum as a very young child. It was terrifying. Not only did I feel completely out of control, but I was confused and frightened about what was happening to me. Mainly I was worried that I was causing everyone around me problems and that they would hate me. I felt bad about my behavior, yet as hard as I tried I could not seem to gain control of myself. I think that my eyes must have been wide open with fear. I probably thought I was going to die, I felt so bad. I remember being especially afraid that people would abandon me because I was such a bad little person. And over and over again, as hard as I tried, I could not seem to regain composure. As far as I can remember, my tantrums would begin with my wanting to tell my mother something important that I thought she needed to know about me. And then very quickly things deteriorated, and I got out of control.

As I grew into an adult, the times that felt similar to those early childhood tantrum memories were arguments with my life partner. Something about the atmosphere felt similar. I would want to tell the person something important about me, things would deteriorate, and then I would become very emotional, while my partner would seem to become calmer and calmer. All the while during the altercation I would feel afraid of abandonment, certain that I was unlovable and unbearably bad. It took many years of self-reflection, therapy, and self-alteration not to feel that way any longer.

When my first marriage ended, I was desperately sad. All my dreams were shattered, and I felt a complete failure. Feeling the sadness well up in me like a horrible pain, I went over to see my good friend Melinda. She and I were both in our late twenties. Melinda had a son like mine, age two at the time. We had met because our two sons played together in the neighborhood playground near our homes. I lay on her large water bed and cried and cried. She sat with me and rubbed my back, saying soothing things like, "Oh, oh, this must be so very painful for you, Tamar," as if talking to a young child. Suddenly her little toddler entered the room and stood and stared at us. She explained to him very softly, "Tamar is very sad and sore. Oh, oh, so sore." He repeated what she said in his sweet little voice, "Oh, oh, so sore, so sore, Mommy?" She nodded her head, and he left the room satisfied with her explanation. I always remembered the kindness Melinda showed me and her son that night, but more specifically, I remember how she taught her son acceptance of sorrow. When I left to return to my home later that night, I felt as if I had been wrapped in a huge warm blanket of love. I felt safe and calm. I slept like a baby, ready to wake up the next day and face my new life as a single parent. This is how I want children to feel after they have worked through their tantrums with me.

When a young child has a tantrum, I see myself in him immediately. I remember all the fear and confusion, and I imagine that the child is feeling similar kinds of things. Therefore, I do not threaten abandonment to a small child who is flailing about uncontrollably. I say things like, "I am going to stay right here by you until you feel more in control of yourself. I will not leave you. I am not angry with you." Sometimes, I add, "I love you. You are okay with me." I mean what I say. I do not expect the child to calm down because I know that as hard as he might try, he cannot stop doing what he is feeling. He does not mean any harm to me. He has just, plain and simply, lost control of himself emotionally. When he becomes calm again, we will be able to talk about what happened to him. During the tantrum the child is far too emotional for any type of rational conversation. If he allows me, I will hold him through the tantrum so that he does not hurt himself or others. If not, I will accompany him to a quiet area where we can be together safely until his tantrum subsides. I stay with him for as long as it takes.

It does not matter to me what the reason for the tantrum is. I have sat with a four-year-old child who witnessed his mother murdered by his father. He was sent to live with his grandmother when his father went to jail. Each day, at a certain moment, for what teachers often call "no apparent reason," this little boy would lose complete control and fall into an indescribable tantrum of confusion, rage, and sorrow. The only way out was through it, and we would go into a private room where I stayed with him until his emotional storm subsided. Sometimes it would take ten minutes, or it might last for longer than forty minutes. On a lighter note, I have accompanied young children who enter into tantrums because they did not receive the toy they wanted to play with. I address it in exactly the same way as with the child whose experience was deeply traumatic. I stay with them until they have worked it through, making sure they do not hurt themselves or others. Mostly I am quiet with them, but every now and again I might tell them that they are with me and that I will not leave them.

I have never been able to work out why teachers become so angry with children who have tantrums. I cannot understand why they think young children are manipulating them or seeking attention in a way that is harmful. Believe me, I can tell you from personal experience that having a tantrum is no fun. Nor have I ever met a child who enjoys having one. They all seem frightened and confused. They may have started out enraged, but then I believe they feel so bad about themselves for having angry feelings in the first place that they deteriorate into an uncontrollable tantrum. As a teacher, it is my responsibility to guide children through these turbulent feelings with compassion, understanding, and acceptance. It is the only way to help them break out of the cycle of thinking they are bad people for having confusing feelings, wants, needs, and desires.

Toddlers

I cannot conclude a chapter about discipline strategies without a short note about toddlers. So often I hear them called "terrible twos." I understand where that name comes from. It is, indeed, a challenging period of a child's life and even more challenging for the adults who care for children. Truly, from eighteen months to approximately three years of age children go through a very confusing time. They are pulled in two directions emotionally. The first is to become more mature and independent, and the second is to be as dependent on the adults around them as they were as infants. It is termed the period of "rapprochement." As the toddler's cognitive and physical skills develop, so too does her realization that she is separate from those she loves. For the adult who is caring about and educating this child, suddenly it seems as if the sweet little infant who needed us a few days ago has suddenly turned into a freedom-fighting monster! Then again, just when we are becoming used to the child becoming independent and separate, suddenly she turns around and needs us all over again, sinking into our lap with thumb in mouth, resting her head wearily against our chest. Weary from life's battles, weary from being big and independent—she's needing a rest from it all, needing to gather confidence from the adults around her once again. Instead of rejoicing that this mighty toddler has learned to defiantly say no, we become outraged and hurt. I sometimes think that when we are faced with those amazing two-year-olds, we become toddlers ourselves again!

I can make three suggestions based on what has helped me when I work with this age group of children:

- Choose your battles. Let go of those challenges that are less important. Safety first.
- Do not use long preachy sentences. Very young children will not be concentrating on that long sermon about how to behave. They will have moved on after the first few words. Keep it clear, firm, and simple.
- Remember: not long ago they were infants.

In fact, this is one of the most important times of our lives for understanding separation and autonomy.

Try to think back to when you were a toddler. What do you remember about that time in your life? What was challenging about it? If you cannot remember by yourself, interview family members to find out what they recall. Perhaps they will describe that you were a very difficult child. Ask how they dealt with the challenge that was you! Chances are, that period of your life has influenced how you deal with separation and autonomy now as an adult. Understanding our own issues with separation and independence can help us work with children who are learning this important lesson. It will make a difference in how we understand what it feels like to be a toddler and whether we see them as "terrible" or accept them as "freedom fighters."

ACTIONS TO TAKE

Find Out about Other People's Strategies

When I was in my first year as a preschool teacher, our supervisor from the Ministry of Education took teachers like me on field trips to visit and observe other classrooms in different schools. I loved those excursions to see the ways more experienced teachers were creating curriculum or managing behaviors. I learned many different strategies.

One time I returned to my classroom feeling most uncomfortable and frustrated. I thought, "How could I ever become as experienced and do such wonderful things as I saw the teacher do today?" I must have looked very crestfallen, because my supervisor asked me what was troubling me. I told her about my frustrations and yet how much I enjoyed learning from these teachers. "Could I ever be as good as them?" I asked her wistfully. I remember her smile these thirty years later. It was full of wisdom and understanding. She replied that this type of frustration was healthy and productive because it showed I had passion, commitment, and the will to change. She felt sure that I would be a fine teacher one day.

Seeking out other people's strategies is a wise thing to do, even if it makes you feel frustrated because you are not yet able to do the things you see others capable of doing with apparent ease. Take that frustration to be healthy and productive, because it means that you aspire to change and are committed to excellence. Everyone has ideas that are different from yours. They have probably learned from other people too. And everyone's life experience influences his or her personal style and choice of strategies. Some of the ways others interact with children might not feel right for you, even though they seem effective at the time. As an adult, you can choose which strategy is right for you by connecting it to your own childhood experiences, reading about current practices and research in the field, or discussing it with your peers.

Reading about classroom management strategies is helpful, but visiting other teachers' classrooms and observing their interactions can be beneficial as well. Sometimes seeing a teacher modeling different behaviors or strategies gives you a concrete image of how it can be done. As a college professor, one of my duties is to regularly observe my colleagues and write an observation report for their portfolio. They do the same for me. I love watching them teach. Almost every time I learn a new or slightly different strategy to add to my repertoire as a teacher educator. For example, the last time I observed one of my colleagues using PowerPoint effectively, it gave me the courage, the final push, to start using it appropriately and successfully in my classes. Something about the ease with which she handled the technology showed me that I could do it too!

Remember How You Felt as a Child

Think back to your early childhood, and try to remember the times you felt most helpless. How did you deal with it? What types of life decisions were made for you without consulting you? As a child, how were you allowed or supported to process grief, fear, or anger? What ways did you develop to feel in control? How did you seek attention as a child, and now as an adult how do you react to children who want your attention? How did you feel when you had a tantrum? Who helped you work through it? How were you allowed to express feelings? What was considered disrespectful by your parents? What was confusing for you about the significant adults in your life? How did you know you were loved? How did your family express fear or deal with separation? Where and with whom did you feel emotionally safe?

CONCLUSION

In this chapter I have shared some strategies or suggestions that have worked for me. Perhaps some of them make sense to you and could be supportive in your work with young children. On the other hand, you might find them unsuited to who you are. Check out your emotional responses to my suggested strategies while reflecting on the following:

- Ways of disciplining vary from family to family. Some might have worked for you; others you have decided to do differently.
- What affected your parents when they disciplined you? What affected you? Mostly our parents wanted what was best for their children. They learned ways of disciplining through generations of parenting or through cultural norms. Our parents did not always know what to do. They were not born parenting experts, and they constantly felt guilty that they weren't good enough parents. How could they not? They were always being told what to do or educated about the best way to parent by family members, teachers, principals, school counselors, pediatricians, television, newspapers, radio talk shows, books, and magazines.
- As a teacher, how has your discipline style been influenced? What decisions will you make? Why? What is your bottom line? What is your philosophy about life? How did you develop your beliefs or values? What do you think about when you think about discipline?

And remember:

- The way you were disciplined will affect how you react to children—either you will want to do it differently, or it worked for you!
- Strategies that worked for me might not work for you. I think back to one of my dissertation advisers, a grief counselor. He had a baseball cap in his office with a saying written across the front of it: Take my advice, I don't use it!

References

Carey, B. 2007. Bad behavior does not doom pupils, studies say. *New York Times*, November 13, http://www.nytimes.com/.

Elkind, D. 2007. Instructive discipline. *ExchangeEveryDay*, September 5, www.childcareexchange.com/eed/issue.php?id= 1806 (accessed March 20, 2008).

Gartrell, D. 2004. *The power of guidance: Teaching social-emotional skills in early childhood classrooms*. Clifton Park, N.Y.: Delmar Learning.

Goodall, J. 2006. *My life with the chimpanzees*. Revised edition. New York: Aladdin Paperbacks.

Jacobson, T. 2003. *Confronting our discomfort: Clearing the way for anti-bias in early childhood*. Portsmouth, N.H.: Heinemann.

Kidjo, A. 2007. Gimme shelter. On *Djin Djin*. CD. Razor and Tie/ Starbucks Entertainment.

Raines, S. 1995. *Never ever serve sugary snacks on rainy days: The official little instruction book for teachers of young children*. Beltsville, Mass.: Gryphon House.

CHAPTER SEVEN

WE CAN CHANGE OUR EMOTIONAL SCRIPTS

In this moment, it becomes possible for the daughter to create the mother she feels she has always needed and deserved. She re-creates her real mother or she creates a symbolic mother to hold and foster her psychological and emotional development. . . . It is an act that requires an enormous maturity on the daughter's part, an ability no longer to be bound by the conflicts and disappointments of the past, a recognition that change between mother and daughter is still possible although both the child and the mother of childhood have long since vanished.

—KIM CHERNIN

Poems or inspirational quotations are important for me when I am engrossed in the busy day-to-day world of living and working. They serve as important reminders and, in a few words, sum up new and different scripted messages in my brain that slowly but surely replace the old ones that are no longer necessary.

Many years ago when I was in graduate school, my statistics instructor started the lesson by reading us a short inspirational message. Tom Frantz was an excellent statistics professor, and he was also a grief counselor. From time to time he would either start the class or interrupt us in the middle to read a poem or inspirational quotation. It was a moment in time when I was able to gather my thoughts within—like taking a deep breath for the brain and soul—and then return to the matter at hand, in that case, statistics. On one particular night many years ago, Tom Frantz read us the poem "Autobiography in Five Short Chapters" by Portia Nelson:

I

I walk down the street.
*   There is a deep hole in the sidewalk.*
*   I fall in*
*   I am lost . . . I am helpless*
*   It isn't my fault.*
It takes forever to find a way out.

II

I walk down the same street.
*   There is a deep hole in the sidewalk.*
*   I pretend I don't see it.*
*   I fall in again.*
I can't believe I am in the same place.
*   but, it isn't my fault.*
It still takes a long time to get out.

III

I walk down the same street.
There is a deep hole in the sidewalk.
I see it is there.
I still fall in . . . it's a habit.
my eyes are open.
I know where I am.
It is my fault.
I get out immediately.

IV

I walk down the same street.
There is a deep hole in the sidewalk.
I walk around it.

V

I walk down another street.

FACING OUR EMOTIONAL HISTORY CAN BE TOUGH, BUT THAT IS HOW WE MOVE FORWARD.

Becoming aware of my emotional development and history has not always been easy. Facing painful memories is not pleasant or comfortable. When I tell my story, however, I not only take ownership of what happened to me but also validate my experience for myself. Each time I face down those old emotional wounds, it becomes easier to forgive the past and move on positively and constructively. Naturally, when I confront painful memories, I am liable to feel angry toward the adults who took care of me when I was young. Yet, as I examine and explore all that transpired, ask

questions, and probe and pry into my history, I come to the conclusion that everyone did the best they could with what they had
at the time. This process is not about blame. It has everything to
do with understanding and self-acceptance. Armed with an understanding of how I came to feel the way I do, I am able to let go of
past anger and take responsibility for the choices I make as an adult
here and now.

In the past, I preferred to explore my childhood one-on-one
with a professional counselor or therapist. Partly it had to do with
feeling ashamed about exposing my vulnerabilities and anxieties. I
was able to uncover those parts of me only in a safe environment
with someone neutral I could trust. Now that I am older, I do not
feel as much shame as I did when I was young. A couple of years
ago I wrote about significant incidents in my childhood in my blog.
It became important for me to tell my story for others to read along
with me, because it was difficult for me to believe that what had
happened to me as a child had been hurtful. It was painful, and I
cried as I wrote. But each time after I reread the journal entries,
the pain dissipated. In its place came an understanding about how
I had developed emotionally and why I had made the life choices I
had made. I felt liberated and redeemed. Sharing my emotional history helps me become more compassionate and accepting of other
people's pain and confusion. Ultimately it enables me to become
more understanding about children's challenging behaviors, whether they are quiet and withdrawing, aggressive or anxious. When I
reach into my memories and open up what I remember about the
child I once was, I become more competent at emotionally supporting all types of children in my care.

Uncovering my emotional history has taken years to process.
I have worked hard at researching myself, using many different
methods: journaling, meditation, the guidance of an experienced

therapist, reading, and studying. I also include teaching young children and adult students and counseling families in that list. Lately I think I have developed a pretty good picture of the child who was me. I have a clearer understanding of some of the events in my life that affected my perception of self. As I acknowledge memories of early experiences, I am able to separate out those feelings I developed as a child from my adult reality of today. What follows is my emotional story, as I remember and understand it. Within it lies the secret to the message that my brain developed about myself. In order to change or relearn that scripted message, I first had to understand how it happened. I tell it to you in the hopes that through my example you might find your own way to uncover your emotional history and—if you want—change the scripted message you developed about yourself.

I Tell My Story

I was the product of a very brief, stormy marriage, wedged between two others that were considered more important. I was way too little (four years old) to be blamed for all my mother's feelings of insecurity, confusion, guilt, fear, or low self-worth during those first years, which were occupied with her divorcing my father and marrying my stepfather. And yet, there I was, born and delivered, and feeling always that I belonged neither here nor there, feeling in the way as my mother proceeded on to the third marriage. I remember the love between my mother and stepfather as passionate. They were sometimes full of rage and fought often. At other times, they were loving and excited. When I was little, I remember being worried about how my mother was feeling. When she was sad or anxious, I remember feeling afraid. When she was happy, I felt safe.

My mother constantly reminded me not to make too much noise, eat too much food—not to do this, that, or the other in case I disturbed, troubled, or burdened my new stepfather. Indeed, I remember working hard not to annoy him. And yet life was happening to me too. I was, after all, a young, vibrant child, curious, thinking, feeling, and growing. Sometimes I wanted to be heard. I yearned for attention, and I let them know it! But, oh dear, when that happened the wrath seemed merciless—it knew no bounds. It took the form of yelling, threatening, slapping, and, much more terrifying for me, my mother's uncontrollable sobbing as she accused me of "destroying her" and "ruining her life." As she would weep, I would feel as if I were spiraling down, sinking into a dark abyss of shame and terror, longing for her love, terrified of losing it, of losing her, ashamed of all the pain I was causing. I would try to hug her and apologize. Mostly I did not know what I was apologizing for, and I was desperate to make everything right again, in any way I knew how. She would turn her head and body away from me. She would stiffen from my touch. I would leave notes everywhere for her to find, begging forgiveness, promising to be good, saying I would never do whatever it was I did again. She did not reply to those notes or soften in response to my anguish and terror. Over time, a script began to develop in my brain, recurring, repeating, reinforcing, confirming my belief in myself: "I am unlovable, a burden, in the way, to blame, at fault. I destroy people, ruin their lives, and, deep down, I am oh so bad, evil perhaps, worthless, undeserving."

When I was eight years old, my younger brother was born. One night, I was restless, could not sleep, and wanted to go to the bathroom. My stomach was churning, and I became fearful. Mother came up to my bedroom and insisted I go to sleep. I could not. I called her again and again. Finally she dragged me out of my bed, slapping and beating me, hurling me around the room, yelling at me to be quiet, to go to sleep, telling me over and over that I was disturbing her husband and waking the new baby, who was asleep in their bedroom downstairs. At one point, her yells and my screams of terror brought a neighborhood police officer, who was going about his rounds, to the window. "Everything all right in there, madam?" he asked. She said that all was well and returned to my room yelling at me, "Now look what you've done. The police came here because of your performance!" She returned to her room.

Still unable to sleep, I stumbled as softly as I could down the stairs and lay on the sofa in the living room, as near as possible to her closed bedroom door. At the time, we lived behind my stepfather's store, a long, dark warehouse turned into a home. My mother had painted the back wall a deep shade of red, and as there were no windows, I always remember the living room as being long, dark, and ominous. As I lay down, I sensed a large, thick, pungent, pale green, cobweb like cloud above my head, spreading out over the ceiling, with layers falling down and around to hover just above my body. I was terrified and lay awake trembling, not daring to call out, keeping my eyes fixed on that imaginary cloud until the morning light drove it away.

The next day, as I struggled in the bathroom, my mother screamed out in a panic while she pulled out of me the longest, thickest tapeworm you have ever seen! I was rushed to the hospital, where I spent a few days being cared for by Irish nuns. Their kindness bathed and healed me. I remember the hospital as being light and airy, nuns dressed in white habits, goodness shining and showering all around. I remember, too, feeling grateful and safe. I loved the food they brought me. I did not want to return home. My mother has since told me that she very much regretted that incident, but how could she have known that my restlessness that night was caused by a tapeworm? She just thought I was being naughty.

The incident, in and of itself, would not have been so memorable or frightening had it not played into my mother's constant fear of disturbing her husband and her anxiety about the success of her third marriage. Mostly what I remember was the terror from making all that trouble and disturbing my baby brother and stepfather asleep in their room. After all, I loved my mother dearly and wanted to please her in every way possible. Thus, the incident became a symbol for me, a concrete confirmation of the scripted message I was internalizing about myself, my belief that "I am unlovable, a burden, in the way, to blame, at fault. I destroy people, ruin their lives, and, deep down, I am oh so bad, evil perhaps, worthless, undeserving."

As I grew up, I found myself over and over again loving people way more than they loved me. I went out into the workforce, and no matter how hard I tried at whatever I took on, with hours of labor, effort, or devotion, I could not help but feel that old message repeating itself like a meditation mantra. Like that thick, pale green, pungent, cobweblike cloud, the feeling of worthlessness hovered above my head over and over again. And so I learned to run. I ran away instead of holding still and confronting the pain. I ran from marriages, friends, family, workplaces, education. The more I ran, the more shame I felt—and, therefore, the more I reinforced the script I had developed.

Then one day, more than twenty years ago, I started to break the cycle. I remember the moment it happened. I was sitting behind a wooden slatted screen in a tiny neighborhood synagogue near my home in Israel, listening to the sounds of my thirteen-year-old son as he sang loud, sweet, and clear, like a lark ringing through the rafters. He was surrounded by his father and his father's family as he was initiated into the Jewish community, recognized as an adult-to-be. Watching my beautiful son that day of his Bar Mitzvah, flanked by strangers and my self-made community of supporters, somewhere deep inside me a voice trembled and stirred. It whispered, "You are not all that bad, Tamar. You deserve more out of life." Although my mothering days were certainly not over, my son was now initiated into the adult world. I felt that it was time for me to acquire a higher education and seek out who I wanted to be. The old pattern of belief about myself started to crumble away that moment in the synagogue.

I carried myself and my old scripted message, struggling in and out of confidence, across the seas to the United States as I set out on my new journey. I charged forward, with a miraculous kind of inner hope and courage, once again surrounded and supported by loving strangers and a self-made community of supporters. I studied and worked long, hard hours, putting my son through college, acquiring three degrees, and writing a book. With my therapist's help I learned to hold still, cease the running, and confront my pain head on. Bit by bit I started to break down that old belief that still, at times, can send me spiraling into my old dark abyss of shame. Nowadays, I allow myself to feel lovable and deserving of my life partner, my son, and my professional colleagues. I do still have to work on those feelings that I am "evil perhaps, worthless, and undeserving," but mostly they are like old battered wounds that awaken with the rain.

Rewriting the Scripted Message

I am sure that you have a story to tell too. Maybe it is more painful than mine—perhaps not as painful. Whatever it is, your emotional history has affected who you have become and the choices you make in your personal and professional life. When I read over my story now, so many years later, I realize how anxious and fearful my mother must have been as she tried to find love and the right way to keep all the different pieces of the family together. Her own childhood was not easy by any means. She suffered and struggled through many difficult times. She worked hard in her way to be the best mother she could be. I have had my moments of anger and anguish thinking of little Tamar trying to please her mother and being constantly afraid. But now I am an independent adult and understand that those scripted messages I internalized are not the truth about me, not the reality of who I am. As I uncover the layers of emotional memory and realize my vulnerabilities and weaknesses, I am able to rewrite my script to reflect what I am actually capable of.

In coming to understand my own childhood, my emotional history, I have realized that all young children are affected emotionally by the way they are treated. They need support and guidance as they internalize and interpret the messages they receive from significant adults in their lives—namely, parents, extended family members, teachers, and so on. As teachers of young children it is our responsibility to work hard at supporting children through this process. We can do this by being authentic, honest, and open; by creating safe emotional spaces so that children can share their deepest feelings with us; and, most importantly, by understanding ourselves. For it is by understanding our emotional history that we are able to rewrite those messages we developed about ourselves early on.

It is critical for children that we allow them opportunities and give them different options for the scripted messages they are developing about themselves. For example, if some learn that the only way to be acknowledged is through violence or punishment, they will do everything they can to confirm that message. We have a chance, as their teachers, to do it differently. Just because we might have been hurt by our families does not mean we have to repeat the pattern with others. We have a choice about what we do. In turn, we can help the children in our care realize that too. Our greatest gift as educators is to offer children a different option from what they have already learned.

I remember a substitute teacher coming into my office distraught and in complete disarray. Her hair was tangled, her clothes disheveled, her cheeks flushed, and her breathing heavy. She described the behavior of a four-year-old child in the classroom and how she had engaged him in a physical battle of wills. When she had finished telling me about the hitting, kicking, spitting, scratching, and biting that had occurred while she tried to hold him down to the floor, I stared at her and said, "Good Lord! How on earth did you let it get so out of hand?" She could have called for help at any time. It turned out that she was determined to "tame" him, as she described it. She was not going to let him have the last word or power over her. She felt as if she would fight him to the last breath if she had to! In this interaction, the teacher believed absolutely that the child was at fault and that she was going to be the one to set him straight. When I visited the child in the classroom, he was still angry and resentful. He was as flushed and disheveled as the teacher. I wondered why or how the teacher had forgotten that the child was a four-year-old—just a small boy. The only power he had was to bite and scratch when he was clearly feeling threatened about his very survival. He must have been terrified when she held him down with all her power. I wondered what that teacher's personal emotional story could be to make her want to fight a small child as if "to the last breath." I never found out because she left our center soon after that.

When I understand my emotional story, I become more intentional in the disciplinary choices I make and am able to monitor my reactions—unlike the time I spanked my son because of the shame I was feeling about being a single parent. I always used to be afraid that people would find out how bad I am. Until I was able to break through that old belief I had developed about being a troublemaker, I found myself hesitant and weak, unable to make decisions, and quite hopeless at setting clear boundaries. I was constantly worrying about pleasing people, and I was focused on not allowing them to know the *real* me. Naturally this affected all my relationships in my personal life. Professionally, it got in the way of my work with children. The less afraid I became, the clearer I could be with children and their families. I notice that even now when I read evaluations students write about the effectiveness of my courses or teaching, I sometimes feel a hint of anxiety niggling at me deep down that reiterates whispers of the old message, "Oh dear, they will surely realize how bad I am now!" I am forever feeling relieved when my work is acceptable or acknowledged. Sometimes it almost feels as if I have been saved from a death sentence at the last minute—until the next time!

By allowing myself to uncover my emotional history, I become more inclined to accept and acknowledge that children all have a unique story to tell. Each child's level of sensitivity and resilience is different. Some children suffer so much more abuse than I ever encountered in my life. And yet they seem capable of letting go of memories or not allowing them to dictate who they become.

In fact, they develop strength in the face of adversity. They learn quickly not to need acknowledgment from significant adults in their lives. Others are more sensitive and feel hurt by the slightest offensive interaction. I have seen small children who dissolve into tears from one angry look or a brusque "tsk-tsk" from their caregiver or parent. There is no one right way to be. But it is as important to understand the child's emotional history as it is to know our own. It is like learning a different language.

I will never forget the day my therapist said to me, "Nothing you could do or say in this room could make me leave you. I am not afraid of you." I sat glued to my chair, a grown woman in her fifties, trying to allow his words to seep into my brain and drive out the old message of how bad I thought I was. It took months for me to digest his meaning and, finally, to emotionally accept what he was saying to me. His words spoke straight to the core of my self-identity. They stopped me in my tracks and allowed me to hold still with myself. He had learned my language. Mind you, I had been saying those sorts of things to young children for years, because I had recognized those emotional scripts developing in their brains. Changing the pattern in young children works so much more quickly than in adults.

It Is All about Emotions

In the end, I must disagree with my colleague who says, "It's all about behavior management." I do not only manage children's behaviors. I help them negotiate their feelings. I learn their emotional history and understand what kinds of messages they are internalizing in their brains—and why. And it all begins with my relationship with myself. I observe and learn what moves, frightens, and comforts me. Uncovering feelings I learned to repress or hide, I explore the kinds of messages that I internalized as a young child. Bit by bit I befriend my shadows: fears, shame, guilt, vulnerabilities, and attitudes I have interpreted as weaknesses. I find my voice and become strong, confident, and assertive, accepting of all the different pieces of myself. I develop compassion for how I came to be the person I am now. I learn to love myself unconditionally. And then I transfer this same kind of relationship onto the children in my care.

I think of Tom Frantz back in 1991, when he said that "we teach that which we need to learn." He asked us to explain why we had decided to take his course on grief counseling, and he warned us not to give a "baloney reason." He said, "Don't say it is because you like to help people or something like that. Try and think more deeply about why you feel you want to take this course." After I had worked out the *real* reason for my choosing to take his course (and that is a long story for a different time, for a different book perhaps), I also realized that I had chosen to teach young children so that I would learn about my own childhood. Even more important than that, working with children has enabled me to redeem my inner child and relearn the scripted messages I internalized in my childhood.

Each time I understand a young child's emotional needs, I learn something new about myself. Back and forth between child and teacher, we are able to share our scripted messages, our pain and humiliation, our joy and exuberance. Something about the lonely, frightened child in me was able to reach out and redeem itself through the tender, open, loving, vulnerable neediness of the young children I taught. I have a favorite photograph of myself when I was a young toddler. I am sitting wearing a pretty dress and holding a doll upside down. There is a mischievous, joyous twinkle in my eye, and I am smiling. I love to look at that photograph, for it reminds me that within us all there is a joyous, playful, childlike soul. It only becomes heavy when weighed down by messages we receive from complex, well-intentioned, anxious adults around us. My responsibility as a teacher or caregiver is to help young children preserve their twinkle, their joy and natural curiosity. I do that best by allowing myself to rediscover my own. And then, together, we can rewrite our emotional scripts.

Recently, Sharon, a graduate student, wrote in her final paper, "The greatest early educators must still be children, in everything they do. Some personality trait that makes these teachers who [they are] . . . gives the teacher the magic and wonder to work with young children."

ACTIONS TO TAKE

Write Your Script

The way in which you choose to research yourself depends on you. For some, it is helpful to have a therapist, mentor, or spiritual leader accompany them and bear witness to the self-exploration journey. For others, it might be more beneficial to go it alone or with a support group. Some learn through education classes and by reading books. I have known people to uncover important memories in the space of a one-hour workshop, through journaling or meditation. Sometimes the journey is straightforward with continual progress. At other times the road twists and turns, and we find ourselves going back a few steps to relearn or understand something we learned from a different angle or perspective.

Through the Internet I have met many people who write their private ruminations in blogs for others to read. Many people have written their most personal stories in books for the world to read. I have gathered courage and learned much about myself by reading memoirs of people who have overcome abusive childhoods. As much as I realize just how resilient we all are, I am aware that abusive interactions, whether physical or emotional, take their toll on young children and remain in their emotional memory to affect every aspect of their lives as they grow into adults.

Take me, for example. Here I am, an accomplished author and professor of early childhood. I have strong and constant relationships with all sorts of people, including my life partner, my son, family members, friends, and colleagues. I am financially able to provide for myself and my son and seem quite successful to people who know me. Nevertheless, on an emotional level, I am often anxious and unsure of myself. I have never really slept well and have great difficulty in believing that I am lovable or worthy of anything. While I am able to make a stand for others, I find it very difficult to fight for myself. I have to work hard at subduing voices in my brain that constantly tell me how bad, destructive, overweight, ugly, or old I am. These voices say I am a fraud and a failure. Even though I am aware that how I feel about myself comes from the messages I received as a child, emotionally life is a struggle. I am often exhausted from just being me! This tells me that we are not all quite as resilient as we think or as we seem to others.

Writing your script can help you see, in black and white, detached from your inner ruminations, a map of who you were, are, and are becoming. From time to time you will be able to read what you wrote years before. I am always excited to see how I have developed. I remain curious to work out why I might not have progressed. Writing your life script becomes a concrete way to change beliefs you learned about yourself as a child.

Here for you to ponder are some ideas or questions about what influenced your emotional development. Interviewing family members can be helpful as you write your life script.

- In the birth order for your family where were you, and how did that affect relationships within the family?

- What became your role in the family? For example, were you considered the good person, responsible and caring; the family clown, irresponsible and challenging; a martyr; a bohemian; a hippie; a saint; a victim; the bad seed? I am sure you can think of your own names for the roles of people in your family.

- Which life challenges affected your parents or guardians that might have influenced their interactions with you?

- What situations or incidents (if any) were especially notable or memorable for you? Why do you think they were symbolic or particularly traumatic for you?

- What were some of the myths or stories told over and over again about you, your siblings, or, for that matter, any of your family members?

- What were some of your losses growing up? What separations did you experience: divorce, death, emotional abandonment, moving to new homes or to different states or countries?

- How did you acquire your gender identity? Who were your major influences or role models? What was enjoyable, frustrating, exciting, or frightening about becoming a woman or a man?

- What were life scripts of your parents, guardians, or extended family members that might have influenced you? For example, I heard my maternal grandmother's story many times. It was wild and dramatic, including tales of tragedy, death, disappointment, and abandonment. I believe that her story, filtered through my mother and aunt, had an impact on me, so that "suffering is honorable" became a theme for my life. I discovered all that by creating a genogram (an in-depth family tree) both during therapy and as an assignment for a family therapy course I took in graduate school. As I wrote about each person's version of my grandmother's story, I recognized that I had emotionally taken on some of her life script of being an orphan and abandoned—two or three generations later. Indeed, interviewing family members is crucial for this type of self-exploration.

- How does your life script affect your ability to accept diversity? While this is a much larger topic, which I explored in depth in *Confronting Our Discomfort*, it is important to remember that our life scripts and early childhood experiences affected not only our emotional development but also how we learned about our cultural identity and how to accept differences in others (Jacobson, 2003).

66 When we confront bias, we touch the core of a person's being. It is connected to significant people in our lives. Society, including media, schools, and communities, influences bias as well. However, it is especially personal and close to family members when we were very young. They taught us to

discern what is good and evil, right and wrong. We remember their words even after we have grown into adults, 'This is the way it's got to be. Otherwise it is very dangerous, so be careful!' They warn us of all the terrible things that may happen to us if we are not careful in our relationships with people different from us. " (Jacobson 2003, 49)

CONCLUSION

When I relocated to Philadelphia from Buffalo a few years ago, I had to bid farewell to my therapist. I was ready. I had taken a self-researching journey with him as my guide for many years. And what an exciting trip it was! He accompanied me through my explorations as I uncovered my emotional history, and at times he bore witness to my pain as well as my joy and exhilaration at discovering different realities about myself. It was a great experience, enhancing and deepening the quality of my personal and professional relationships in many different ways. As a parting gift, he gave me a small poster with an inspirational quote from Martha Graham, a famous American dancer and choreographer. I framed it and keep it on my bookshelf close to where I work. When I feel myself slipping into my old childhood scripted patterns, I read the words to remind me to gather my thoughts within—like taking a deep breath for the brain and soul. I brush away that ancient thick, pungent, pale green, cobweblike cloud that hung over me when I was eight years old and lying in the dark, ominous living room, so close to the room where the most important person in my life lay, but where I did not dare to call out. I rewrite my emotional script.

" There is a vitality, a life force, an energy, a quickening that
is translated through you into action, and because there
is only one of you in all of time, this expression is unique.
And if you block it, it will never exist through any other
medium and it will be lost. The world will not have it. It
is not your business to determine how good it is nor how
valuable nor how it compares with other expressions. It
is your business to keep it yours clearly and directly, to
keep the channel open. You do not even have to believe in
yourself or your work. You have to keep yourself open and
aware to the urges that motivate you. Keep the channel
open. " (Martha Graham, quoted in De Mille 1991)

References

Chernin, K. 1998. *The woman who gave birth to her mother: Seven stages of change in women's lives.* New York: Penguin.

De Mille, Agnes. 1991. *Martha: The life and work of Martha Graham.* New York: Random House.

Jacobson, T. 2003. *Confronting our discomfort: Clearing the way for anti-bias in early childhood.* Portsmouth, N.H.: Heinemann.

Nelson, P. 1993. *There's a hole in my sidewalk: The romance of self-discovery.* Hillsboro, Ore.: Beyond Words Publishing.

APPENDIX

EARLY CHILDHOOD TEACHER SURVEY

Thank you for participating in this survey. Please be assured that your answers will be kept entirely confidential. Do not put your name anywhere on the questionnaire. In some cases you will be asked to "circle the most appropriate answer for you." In other cases you will be asked to "write in" answers in your own words. The survey should require no more than 10 minutes to complete.

First, we would like to ask you about anger in adults and in yourself.

1) How often do you experience feelings of anger? *(Please check the answer that is appropriate for you.)*

☐   ☐   ☐   ☐   ☐   ☐
Never   Seldom   Occasionally Commonly   Often   Always

2) Please describe what anger feels like to you. *(Use back side of questionnaire if needed.)*

_____

_____

_____

_____

_____

_____

3) Is it bad for adults to be angry? *(Please check the answer that is appropriate for you.)*

☐   ☐
Yes   No

4) Was it okay for you to express anger around your parents when you were a child?

☐   ☐
Yes   No

5) Please explain why it was okay or why it was not okay. *(Use back side of questionnaire if needed.)*

_____

_____

_____

_____

_____

6) What makes you angry? *(Use back side of questionnaire if needed.)*

_____

_____

_____

_____

_____

7) How do you express anger? *(Use back side of questionnaire if needed.)*

_____

_____

_____

_____

_____

_____

**Second, we would like to ask you about anger
in children and about child anger in your classroom.**

8) Is it okay for children to express anger in your classroom?

☐   ☐
Yes   No

9) What do you do when children express anger in your classroom? *(Use back side of questionnaire if needed.)*

_____

_____

_____

_____

_____

10) Is it bad for children to be angry? *(Please check the answer that is appropriate for you.)*

☐   ☐
Yes   No

11) How often do you experience feelings of anger when caring for and educating young children?

☐   ☐   ☐   ☐   ☐   ☐
Never   Seldom   Occasionally Commonly   Often   Always

12) What makes you angry when working with young children? *(Use back side of questionnaire if needed.)*

_____

_____

_____

_____

_____

_____

_____

Finally, we would like to ask you some demographic questions.

13) How long have you worked with young children or teachers of young children?

☐   ☐   ☐   ☐   ☐   ☐

Under 1 Yr.   1–5 Yrs.   5–10 Yrs.   10–15 Yrs.   15–20 Yrs.   Over 20 Yrs.

14) What is your age? _____

15) What is your gender?

☐   ☐

Female   Male

16) What is your ethnic or cultural background?

☐   ☐   ☐   ☐   ☐   ☐

Caucasian   African American   Latino   Asian   Native American   Other

17) Have you completed CDA training?

☐   ☐

Yes   No

18) Please indicate your present level of educational attainment.
(Please check the answer that is appropriate for you.)

    ☐ Some High School   ☐ Completed High School

    ☐ Some College   ☐ Associate's Degree

    ☐ Bachelor's Degree   ☐ Master's Degree   ☐ PhD

Thank you for taking time to participate in this survey!

CPSIA information can be obtained
at www.ICGtesting.com
Printed in the USA
JSHW041303140621
15762JS00002B/5